ROASTER-OVEN COOKBOOK

ROASTER-OVEN

GRAMERCY PUBLISHING COMPANY

New York

Contents

1 ABOUT YOUR ROASTER-OVEN 7

It will add hours of leisure to your day. This chapter gives advice on use and care.

2 HORS D'OEUVRES HOT FROM THE OVEN 17

Select two or three varieties. Serve in small quantities so they keep piping hot in oven.

3 BAKED EGGS, CHEESE, AND PASTA 27

"Fourth meals are fun meals"—for snacks after dinner, and drop in guests, bake these favorites.

4 FISH AND SHELLFISH, OVEN STYLE 37

For quick-baked fish, brush with oil, bake 15–20 minutes at 500°. Use no water in pan. Serve with melted butter.

5 BEEF, LAMB, AND PORK—ROASTS AND CASSEROLES 47

Cook tender cuts by dry heat; less tender ones must be braised, stewed, or simmered in water.

6 BAKED CHICKEN AND OTHER OVEN SPECIALTIES 71

Chicken, turkey, duckling recipes from China, East India, Latin America, and France. American favorites too.

7   **VEGETABLES FOR ALL-IN-ONE PLATE COMBINATIONS**   *85*

Root vegetables as potatoes and beets bake fine. Green ones should be cooked first in boiling water on top of stove.

8   **HOT BREADS, CAKES, AND PIES**   *97*

Only moist breads, not pastry and pies, should be baked as part of an oven meal.

9   **DESSERTS FRESH FROM THE OVEN**   *111*

Puddings and fruits are fine to bake with an oven meal. Try some tonight.

10   **ABOUT YOUR BROILER GRIDDLE**   *121*

Complete meals broiled in minutes! You'll want this worthwhile accessory.

INDEX   *127*

1. *About your roaster-oven*

It will add hours of leisure to your day. This chapter gives advice on use and care.

You'll enjoy the portable electric roaster-oven. With it, you can cook whole meals or complete courses in one operation, saving fuel, time, and work. You save dishwashing too, for handsome casseroles can go right from the oven to the most formal table. And as you probably know by now, oven cooking has a special flavor all its own, so even the simplest and most humble of leftovers, dressed up in a sauce and oven-baked, becomes quite delectable.

TABLE-TOP MEALS ARE MORE CONVENIENT

One of the very special appeals of your electric roaster is its portability. Whether used for all the cooking in a small apartment or country cottage, or to supplement a standard range, this portable appliance makes cooking easier, more convenient. Even at high noon in July, oven cooking is not as humid a task as you would expect, for the roaster does not heat the kitchen. All through the year, the roaster simplifies meal preparation. You need not bend, stoop, and tug to get at foods, for the oven rests on a table top or can be bought with its own special cabinet. Be sure to keep it where it is always and quickly available.

SO MUCH MORE LEISURE

Oven meals in your roaster requires so little attention that you actually add several hours of leisure to your day. Now, when so many of us are working wives and mothers, the extra leisure it affords makes your roaster a truly worthwhile investment. You plug it in wherever you please. Perhaps in a finished basement or playroom. On the porch or in the den . . . for the children or for large gatherings . . . everywhere it goes to work it takes the strain out of cooking, frees you from pot-watching and washing.

HOW TO USE YOUR ROASTER-OVEN

Cook anything in your portable roaster-oven that you would do in larger models: roast meat and fowl perfectly; bake featherlight cakes, cookies, breads, rolls; bake delicious puddings, pies, and vegetables. Here are the do's and don'ts of roaster use:

1. Connect it to a wall outlet on AC current. Do not use other appliances on the same circuit at the same time or you will overload the line.

2. Be sure the oven well is in place. It must be used always.

3. Set the dial to preheat oven to temperature recommended in recipe. I prefer a preheated oven, because cooking can be timed more accurately, roasts brown better. However, it is sometimes more convenient to start in a cold oven, so add 20-30 minutes to total time. Most baking must be done in preheated oven.

4. When light signals that oven is preheated, lower baking dishes, placed on large rack which comes with oven, into the well. Cover quickly and start timing the recipe.

5. Your roaster probably is equipped with a glass viewer so you can check cooking stage without removing cover. Take cover off only when necessary and avoid excessive heat loss.

6. When cooking is done, turn off heat, serve immediately. The oven keeps foods warm for short periods, but for extended delays, set dial at 150°. Check to be sure there is enough liquid in casserole so foods do not dry out. Add more if needed.

7. If your roaster comes with adjustable vents, set at *preheat*, turn to *roast* or *bake* positions when foods go into oven. The larger the opening, the browner the cooking. If the opening is small, steam collects and cooking is easier.

8. The signal light flashes off and on during the cooking operation. This is necessary to keep the oven at temperature for which it is set.

9. If your roaster has a timer, follow manufacturer's directions

for use. It will help you start and stop cooking . . . a marvelous accessory to free you from the kitchen, get you off to a club meeting or out to shop while dinners cook automatically.

SPECIAL USES

You will find so many good uses for your roaster: For picnic fun, carry it wrapped in a blanket and food will stay warm for three or four hours, or even longer. If you are planning a church or club supper, right in the oven well you can prepare steaming hot soup (keep it warm at 250°) . . . bake beans . . . braise chicken . . . scallop potatoes . . . make hot cocoa. When your oven is on anyway or while it is still warm, these thrift tips will help you make the most of it:

1. Save celery tops or parsley, dry them in oven at 150° and use for seasoning soups, salads, and stews.
2. To soften brown sugar, place in warm oven to reach right texture.
3. Make crumbs: put stale bread into warm oven to crisp but not brown. Roll with rolling pin.
4. Warm coffee cakes, pies, breads, for every meal. These little things do make a difference.
5. Use aluminum foil cups to fill every inch of the roaster rack when you're cooking a complete meal. They save wash-up too.

Do not use your oven for canning without consulting the Home Service Department of your local electric company, or the home demonstration agent, State Extension Service, at your State College.

HOW TO CARE FOR YOUR ROASTER-OVEN

Never use another appliance on the same circuit. Never immerse the body of the roaster in water. Handle the well carefully so its fine porcelain surface does not chip. Follow the manufacturer's directions carefully.

AFTER EACH USE

Turn dial off, remove cord from socket. Let roaster cool slightly. Wipe inside and out with damp cloth. Dry. If well is spattered, soak it in warm soapy water, remove it from roaster, and wash and dry at the sink. If it is not spattered, wipe with a damp cloth. Dry thoroughly.

FOR SPECIAL CLEANING

Stubborn spots may be removed by very gentle rubbing with fine steel wool. Dip steel wool in household ammonia first if spots are baked on. Wash with warm soapy water. Dry carefully. Wash rack in hot suds and water. Rinse and dry.

THE INFRA-RED BROILER

This useful accessory is well worth its cost. Use it for quick meals, just as you would any standard oven or other portable broiler. The space around the broiling unit permits air to flow in and out—an essential factor in true broiling which many standard ranges do not have.

Before starting to broil, set the rack into recommended position. Turn on the heat. Only one broiling heat is needed—the distance between the heating coils and food determines cooking speed. In general, large cuts of meat should be broiled as far from coils as possible, so center will be cooked too. Small foods which cook quickly should be set close to the coils.

Never use the cover with your broiler. Never immerse the heating element in water or you will ruin it. See pages 121-126 for special recipes and directions.

THE GRIDDLE

This is the top of your broiling unit. Use it for pancakes, for bacon and eggs, for warming breads and rolls, just as you would any other griddle.

The illustrations which follow give some idea of how to fit casseroles and baking dishes on the rack:

Page 13. *Top row:* Delta blue covered bean pot and casseroles by Red Wing Potteries. *Center:* Covered vegetable pans and meat pan which come with many roasters. (To make a cover for meat pan when braising, not roasting, use aluminum foil.) *Below:* How to place 2 8-inch pie pans.

Page 14. *Top row:* Copper soup kettle, shirring pans, by Vincent A. Savarese. *Center:* Loaf pan and individual casseroles by McKee Glass. Corning Glass (not illustrated) offers wide range of ovenware also. *Bottom:* Handsome enameled, blue Dru-Iron ware baker, pipkin, and oval dish. Many other items are available in this ware.

Page 15. *Top row:* Casserole and chop plate in Starburst pattern by Franciscan Ware; eggplant fills rack. *Bottom:* Stainless steel casserole, underplate, and removable handle by Gense Import. Muffin pan and corn fill the rack.

Page 122. *Top row:* Broiler unit in position on roaster, platter with beaded edge, and frying pan, both by Dru-Iron ware. *Bottom:* Delta coffee pot by Red Wing Potteries, and pie, both kept warm on griddle.

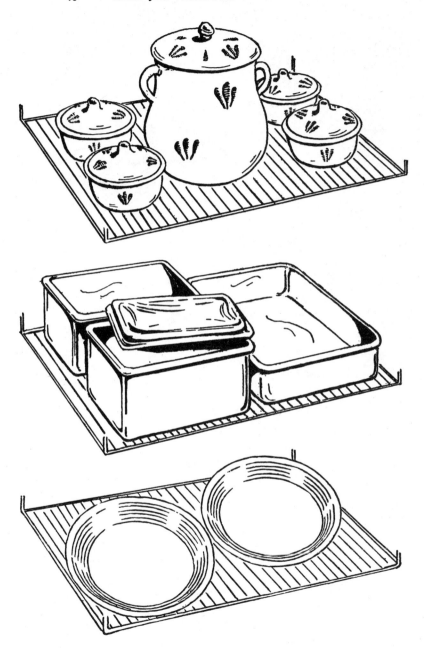

2. *Hors d'oeuvres hot from the oven*

As most hostesses know, hors d'oeuvres take an instant to eat, an eternity to prepare. These are easy, excellent, unexacting. Select one or two as a prelude to an oven meal.

1 CHICKEN LIVER, MUSHROOM AND BACON SKEWERS

Preheat oven to 400° F.
Oven time: 15-18 minutes   *8 skewers*

Cut 4 chicken livers and bacon slices into 4 pieces each. Cut 8 small mushroom caps into equal halves. Using 6-inch skewers, string up alternately 2 pieces of liver, bacon, and mushrooms. Dip in melted butter. Place on rack in shallow baking dish and bake until done. Wind a paper napkin through the skewer ring to serve.

2 BACON AND BURGERS EN BROCHETTE

Preheat oven to 400° F.
Oven time: 15-18 minutes   *1-2 skewers per serving*

Shape twice-ground beef into miniature hamburgers 1-inch in diameter, wrap with half slice of bacon. String each skewer with a stuffed olive, bacon-wrapped burger, tiny cooked white onion, another burger, and finish with an olive. Marinate in French dressing, put on rack in shallow pan and bake until done.

OTHER POSSIBILITIES

Wrap bacon around cooked cauliflower sections and bake until bacon is done. Serve on picks.
Cut a firm green-tipped banana into four chunks. Wrap each chunk in half slice of bacon, secure with toothpick, and bake on baking sheet until bacon is brown.
If these are put into cold oven, allow 20 minutes longer.

Overture: Bake these at the table, and serve with cocktails the night of the pre-theater dinner party.

3   FILLED MUSHROOM CAPS

Preheat oven to 375° F.
Oven time: about 20 minutes   2 caps for each serving

Remove stems from small, clean mushrooms, and save for other uses. Fill caps with chopped cooked chicken and chopped almonds combined with cream and melted butter. Heat in oven on cooky sheet until mushrooms are tender.

4   HAM AND MUSHROOMS IN PASTRY SHELLS

Preheat oven to 375° F.
Oven time: about 12 minutes   12 servings

4 tablespoons butter or margarine
¼ cup finely-chopped onions
1 clove of garlic, mashed
½ cup chopped, cooked ham
½ cup chopped fresh or canned mushrooms
½ cup tomato sauce
3 tablespoons dry sherry wine
24 small pastry shells

Melt butter in saucepan, add onions and garlic and cook until onions are transparent. Stir in ham, mushrooms, tomato sauce and sherry wine. Continue cooking 10 minutes longer until sauce is thickened. Spoon into pastry shells, sprinkle with parsley, and place in oven to get very hot. Keep in oven until needed.

5   COCKTAIL FRANKS IN BLANKETS

Preheat oven to 400° F.
Oven time: 12-15 minutes   Allow 2 franks for each serving

Remove crusts from sliced white bread. Cut bread in half. Spread with mustard. Put a slice of bacon on bottom, bread above it, cocktail frank on top. Roll up, secure with toothpick and bake on rack in shallow pan until bacon is brown.

6   LIVER AND BACON ROLL

Preheat oven to 400° F.
Oven time: about 8 minutes.   Allow 2 rolls for each serving

Grind equal amounts of cooked bacon and liver. Season with salt, pepper, and grated onion. Moisten with oil. Spread on slices of day-old white bread (remove crusts first). Roll up bread and bake on cooky sheet, seam side down, until brown.

7   CHIPPED BEEF BROWNIES

Preheat oven to 400° F.
Oven time: about 8 minutes   Allow 2 for each serving

Cut brown bread into fingers 2½" x 1½" x ½" thick. Finely chop chipped beef, mix with cream cheese and a bit of mayonnaise to make a smooth paste. Spread on bread. Refrigerate until ready to use, then put into oven to brown. Allow 1 cup filling for 15 "brownies." Serve with cocktails.

8   COTTON BLOSSOM CANAPES

Preheat oven to 400° F.
Oven time: about 8 minutes

Grind or chop together 2 parts cooked ham and 1 part chutney. Add Bahamian mustard and chili sauce to make a smooth paste. Spread on toasted bread or crackers, sprinkle with grated cheese and bake on cooky sheet until brown. (One cup of filling makes 15 canapés.)

9   ANCHOVY FINGERS

Preheat oven to 400° F.
Oven time: about 12 minutes

Cut pastry left from making pie shells into fingers 2½" x ½". Spread with butter. Lay 2 anchovy fillets on each finger, put on cooky sheet and bake until brown.

10   SANDWICH SQUARES

Preheat oven to 400° F.
Oven time: about 8 minutes

Spread saltines with butter and grated snappy cheese. Garnish with hard-cooked eggs put through a sieve then mixed with mayonnaise. Put in oven until piping hot.

> *Two favorite hors d'oeuvres featuring a famous product from Switzerland. Serve these with a good red wine, or beer.*

11   SWISS ROLL

Preheat oven to 425° F.
Oven time: 8-12 minutes

Grate ½ pound Swiss cheese and 2 ounces American cheese. Stir in 1 teaspoon Worcestershire sauce, a dash of dry mustard, and 2 slightly-beaten egg yolks. Remove crusts from loaf of day-old white bread. Cut bread into long thin slices. Wrap in damp napkin and let stand in refrigerator for several hours so bread will soften enough to roll. Spread cheese filling on bread, sprinkle with paprika, roll as in jelly roll, cut into thin round slices and bake until brown.

12   SWISS CHEESE AND ONION TART

Preheat oven to 425° F.
Oven time: 8-12 minutes

Cut large Bermuda onion into thin slices, but do not separate into rings. Cook in butter in saucepan until tender. Transfer each slice to piece of pastry dough which is cut in a circle about 4 inches in diameter. Top with a thin matching slice of Swiss cheese. Add another piece of pastry dough, pinch edges together to seal, and bake on baking sheet in hot oven. Another slice of cheese may be put on top of pastry before baking. Cut it no more than 3 inches in diameter so cheese does not run over the sides of the pastry.

Little cheese things for leisurely imbibers.

13   ROQUEFORT CHEESE WAFERS

Preheat oven to 425° F.
Oven time: 12-15 minutes   *Makes about 50 wafers*

1 cup sifted all-purpose flour
1 teaspoon salt
⅛ teaspoon dry mustard
⅓ cup shortening
¾ cup grated Roquefort cheese
3 tablespoons heavy cream

Sift together flour, salt, and mustard. Cut in shortening and cheese until particles are the size of small peas. Add cream, a little at a time, until dough holds together. Roll out ¼-inch thick on a floured board. Use the inside section of your ice-cube tray to cut out wafers. Bake in oven until lightly browned. So good!

14   ROQUEFORT PUFFS

Preheat oven to 425° F.
Oven time: 8-10 minutes   *12 puffs*

¼ pound grated Roquefort cheese
1 egg, slightly beaten
Salt and pepper
12 crackers

Add cheese to egg and mix well. Season with salt and pepper to taste, pile on crackers and bake until cheese puffs up.

GO-TOGETHERS

Bake in 400° oven 12-15 minutes
Roquefort Puffs or Wafers. Recipe 13 or 14.   *Zuppa Del Paes.* Recipe 18, omit grated cheese.

You can be an unruffled hostess if you put a guest in charge of baking these last-minute snacks.

15   CHEESE AND NUT WAFERS

Preheat oven to 400° F.
Oven time: about 8 minutes   *24 wafers*

1½ cups sharp grated cheese
½ cup butter
1 cup sifted all-purpose flour
1 teaspoon salt
½ cup pecan meats

Cream together cheese and butter, then combine with flour and salt until well blended. Refrigerate for several hours. Roll out into 3 rolls about 6 inches long and 2 inches in diameter. Cut off thin slices, put a nut meat in the center of each one and bake on a buttered cooky sheet.

16   CHEESE STICKS

Preheat oven to 400° F.
Oven time: about 15 minutes   *30 sticks*

1 cup sifted all-purpose flour
1 teaspoon baking powder
¼ teaspoon salt
Dash of paprika
1 cup grated sharp cheese
1 egg, slightly beaten
2 tablespoons milk (about)

Sift together flour, baking powder, salt and paprika. Stir in cheese, add egg, and mix well. Spoon in just enough milk to make a somewhat stiff dough. Roll out 1-inch thick on floured board, cut into strips 4 inches long and ¼-inch wide. Bake on cooky sheet.

Best made the day before, reheated and browned in the oven when ready to serve.

17   ONION SOUP

Preheat oven to 400° F.
Oven time: about 15 minutes   *6 servings*

4 tablespoons butter
6 medium onions, cut into thin rings
2 tablespoons flour
Salt and pepper
2 teaspoons prepared mustard
4 cups beef stock, or 4 bouillon cubes dissolved in hot water
½ cup dry white wine
6 slices toast made from French bread
Grated Parmesan cheese

Melt butter in skillet, add onions and cook slowly until they are tender (about 15 minutes). Stir in flour, salt, pepper and mustard. Now pour in stock and wine, and simmer for half an hour. When ready to serve, sprinkle toast with cheese, place in large earthenware casserole or individual soup casseroles, pour soup over toast, and set in oven to brown.

18   ZUPPA DEL PAES

Preheat oven to 400° F.
Oven time: 12-15 minutes   *1 serving*

Pour 1 cup beef stock into an individual earthenware casserole. Toast 1 slice French or Italian bread, spread with butter, and float it on top of soup. Break 1 egg carefully over bread, sprinkle with salt, pepper, and grated cheese. Place in oven until egg sets.

19   CREAMY OATMEAL BREAKFAST CASSEROLE

Preheat oven to 400° F.
Oven time: about 20 minutes   *4 servings*

2 cups quick-cooking oats
4 cups boiling water
1½ teaspoons salt
2 firm bananas (optional)

Measure ½ cup oats and 1 cup boiling water into each of 4 individual casseroles. Season with salt. Slice bananas (if you are
using them) over oats. Cover and bake until oats are creamy-
cooked. You may substitute cooked apricots or prunes, seedless
raisins, chopped dates or figs for bananas. Pass a sugar bowl and
cream too.

20   BAKED SAUSAGES

When you start oven for oatmeal, put sausages in shallow baking
dish. Bake alongside oatmeal until done on all sides. Allow 2
sausages for each serving.

WINTER BRUNCH

Pineapple-Baked Grapefruit. Cut 2 grapefruits in half cross-
wise. Loosen sections by cutting around each one. Pile a
tablespoon or so of crushed pineapple on top, sprinkle
with brown sugar. Bake on rack alongside oatmeal casserole.   *Creamy Oatmeal Breakfast Casserole.* Recipe
19.   *Baked Sausages.* Recipe 20.   *Hot Coffee.*

3. Baked eggs, cheese, and pasta

*Eggs get tough if baked at high temperatures. Automatic
dial keeps heat low.*

21   CASSEROLES FEATURING EGGS

Preheat oven to 350° F.
Oven time: 13-20 minutes   1-2 eggs per serving

Eggs and Walnuts. Sprinkle a greased ramekin with bread
crumbs mixed with grated cheese. Break one or two eggs (the
number depends on the appetite) into it. Season with salt and
pepper. Add 1 tablespoon chopped walnuts and 2 tablespoons
hot condensed cream of mushroom soup which has been diluted
with 1 tablespoon milk. Top with crumbs. Bake in oven until
egg is set.

Eggs with Chicken Livers. Follow recipe above but substitute
cut-up cooked chicken livers for walnuts. Substitute medium
cream sauce for diluted soup.

Cuban Eggs. Follow recipe for eggs and walnuts, but substitute chopped spicy chorizo (Spanish sausage) for nuts, and tomato sauce for cream of mushroom soup.

Eggs Florentine. Drain chopped cooked spinach, put into small
ramekin or custard cup. Make a nest in spinach, drop in melted
butter, and an egg. Bake as above. A delightful low-caloried
luncheon.

HOLIDAY BREAKFAST

Fruit En Brochette. On small skewers, string a canned pine-
apple wedge, maraschino cherry, banana chunk. Repeat
Dip in melted butter, roll in brown sugar. Bake on cooky
sheet with eggs until fruit is glazed and piping hot.
Casserole Featuring Eggs. Select from Recipe 21.   *Hot
Coffee.*

If casserole must stand—and seems to be drying out—add more white sauce and keep hot in oven at reduced temperature.

22   CASSEROLE OF EGGS À LA KING

Preheat oven to 400° F.
Oven time: 15-20 minutes   *6 servings*

1 package (8 ounces) broad noodles, cooked and drained
6 hard-cooked eggs, shelled and quartered
3 tablespoons butter
½ cup chopped onions
½ cup chopped green pepper
¼ cup chopped pimento
¼ cup chopped ripe olives
1 cup medium white sauce
½ teaspoon salt
¼ teaspoon paprika
4 slices white bread

Put cooked noodles into buttered 2-quart casserole. Arrange eggs over them. In a saucepan, melt butter, add onions, green pepper, pimento and olives, and cook until onion is soft but not brown. Stir in white sauce, add salt and paprika, then spoon over eggs in casserole. Cover and bake. Meanwhile trim crusts from bread, cut slices diagonally into triangles and place in oven alongside casserole. (They should brown in about 15 minutes.) When sauce is bubbling, dust again with paprika, remove casserole from oven, tuck buttered toast triangles around it and serve.

LUNCHEON FOR THE CLUB

Casserole of Eggs à la King. Recipe 22.   *Baked Bananas.* Recipe 144. Arrange as spokes radiating from center of dish.   *Sugared Apple Rings.* Cut pared seeded apples into thick rings. Sprinkle with brown sugar. Tuck a green maraschino cherry in each center. Arrange between bananas. Bake together.

23   CURRIED EGGS DIABLO

Preheat oven to 375° F.
Oven time: about 20 minutes   *6 servings*

6 hard-cooked eggs
3 tablespoons light cream
2 teaspoons vinegar
½ teaspoon dry mustard
Salt and pepper
3 tablespoons butter
3 tablespoons flour
2 teaspoons curry power (taste and add more if you wish)
½ teaspoon salt
1½ cups milk
Buttered soft bread crumbs

Shell the eggs, remove yolks, and mash them with cream, vinegar and mustard. Season lightly with salt and pepper. Stuff filling back into eggs, and place them in a buttered 10- or 12-inch baking dish. Make sauce: Melt butter, blend in flour, curry and salt, then slowly add milk. Stir and cook gently until sauce is about texture of thick cream. Spoon over eggs in baking dish, sprinkle with crumbs, and bake until top is lightly brown.

24   LUNCHEON CHEESE BAKE

Preheat oven to 350° F.
Oven time: about 30 minutes   *6 servings*

6 slices buttered white bread, crusts removed
½ pound (2 cups) American cheese, diced
2 eggs, slightly beaten
1 cup light cream
1 teaspoon salt
¼ teaspoon pepper

Cut bread into quarters. Arrange in buttered baking dish. Cover with cheese. Combine eggs, cream, salt and pepper, and pour into dish. Bake until sauce is bubbly. Good with toasted almonds.

25   SUNDAY SUPPER OF CHEESE, OLIVES AND RICE

Preheat oven to 350° F.
Oven time: about 15 minutes   *4 servings*

½ pound sharp Cheddar cheese
1 cup milk
1 egg, slightly beaten
Salt and pepper
2 cups cooked rice
1 cup sliced stuffed olives
3 tablespoons buttered crumbs

In saucepan over low flame, heat cheese and milk. When cheese
has melted, remove from flame and stir in egg. Season with salt
and pepper, then gently add rice. Put a layer of this mixture in
buttered shallow baking dish, add a layer of olives, then repeat
layers. Top with buttered crumbs, and bake uncovered until
sizzling. Serve with hot buttered French bread or crackers.

AFTER A DAY OF GOLF

Sunday Supper of Cheese, Olives and Rice. Recipe 25.
*Garlic Buttered Hot Bread.   Sliced Tomatoes.   Pea-
nut Cookies.* Recipe 134. Bake after removing casserole.
Minty Pineapple Juice.

26   COTTAGE CHEESE AND ONION FONDUE

Preheat oven to 350° F.
Oven time: 20-30 minutes   6 servings

6 medium onions
3 tablespoons butter or margarine
1 cup milk
1 teaspoon salt
4 eggs, slightly beaten
¼ teaspoon pepper
6 slices buttered white bread, crusts removed
1 cup cottage cheese
Dash of paprika
½ cup buttered bread crumbs

Peel and slice onions. In saucepan, combine butter, onions, milk,
salt and pepper. Stew until onions are soft (about 15 minutes).
Remove from heat, and stir in eggs. Arrange bread in greased
shallow baking dish, cover with cottage cheese, top with onion-
egg mixture, sprinkle with paprika and buttered crumbs. Bake
until eggs are set and delicately brown.

27   CHEESE SOUFFLÉ FOR SIX

Preheat oven to 325° F.
Oven time: about 1 hour   6 servings

¼ cup butter
¼ cup flour
1½ cups milk or light cream
1 teaspoon salt
¼ teaspoon freshly grated pepper
2 cups grated sharp cheese
6 egg yolks, well beaten
6 egg whites, beaten until stiff

In saucepan, melt butter, stir in flour, slowly add milk or cream,
salt and pepper. Remove from heat, blend in cheese and egg
yolks. Mix, then fold in egg whites. Pour into ungreased 2-quart
casserole, and bake until firm.

Baked rice is really good as part of an oven meal.

28   BAKED RICE

Preheat oven to 350° F.
Oven time: about 1 hour   *4 servings*

¾ cup raw rice
2 tablespoons butter, margarine or olive oil
2 teaspoons salt
2 cups boiling water or chicken stock
1 tablespoon grated onion

Wash rice. Combine with other ingredients, and pour into greased 1½-quart casserole or oven vegetable pan. Cover and bake until rice is tender.

29   CASSEROLE OF SPANISH RICE

Follow recipe above, but before baking, add 1 cup chopped cooked tomatoes, ½ cup chopped cooked green peppers, 2 tablespoons shredded pimentos, and a dash of chili powder. Chopped cooked giblets or leftover chicken may also be added.

30   SAFFRON RICE

Follow recipe at top of page, but before baking stir in ⅛ teaspoon saffron which has been dissolved in hot water.

31   EAST INDIAN RICE

Before baking, stir into rice 1 teaspoon curry powder. Taste for seasoning; add more curry if needed.

TO KEEP COOKED RICE WARM

Add small amounts of hot water or chicken stock so rice does not dry out.

32   LASAGNE

Preheat oven to 375° F.
Oven time: about 20-25 minutes   *8 servings*

2 tablespoons oil
1 pound chopped beef
4 Italian sausages, cut into 2-inch pieces
2 cloves garlic
2 8-oz. cans tomato sauce
1 No. 2 can (2½ cups) Italian tomatoes
1 6-oz. can tomato paste
1 teaspoon salt
¼ teaspoon pepper
½ teaspoon oregano
½ teaspoon basil
1 8-ounce package lasagne noodles
1 pound Mozzarella cheese, sliced
1 pound ricotta cheese
¾ cup grated Parmesan cheese

Heat oil in a large skillet. Brown beef, sausages and garlic. Discard garlic. Add tomato sauce, tomatoes, tomato paste, salt, pepper, oregano and basil. Cover and simmer for at least an hour. Cook noodles in a large pot of boiling water until just tender. Drain and rinse. In a large casserole place alternate layers of noodles, Mozzarella and ricotta (or cottage) cheeses, meat-tomato sauce, and grated Parmesan cheese. You'll have at least 3 layers of noodles. End with a layer of sauce and Parmesan. Bake uncovered and serve piping hot.

ITALIAN SPECIALTY SUPPER

Lasagne. Recipe 32.   *Tossed Green Salad with anchovies, pimentos, bits of salami or ham.   Italian Bread.* Buy loaf, cut almost through to the bottom, drizzle melted butter and chopped garlic over and between each slice.

33   GNOCCHI

Preheat oven to 400° F.
Oven time: 15-20 minutes   *4 servings*

3 cups milk
¾ cup yellow corn meal
½ teaspoon salt
1 tablespoon butter or margarine
1 egg, slightly beaten
½ cup tomato sauce
3 tablespoons grated cheese
3 tablespoons melted butter

Combine ¾ cup cold milk with corn meal and salt. Heat remaining milk in a saucepan. As soon as milk is hot (do not let boil) stir in cold mush. Cook over low heat until thick (about 10 minutes) stirring frequently. Remove from heat and stir in butter and egg. Spread out in shallow baking dish. Let cool. When firm, cut into 2-inch squares. Arrange in buttered, shallow baking dish. Spoon tomato sauce over squares, then sprinkle with cheese and butter. Bake uncovered until bubbly and slightly brown.

ALL-IN-ONE ROASTER MEAL

Gnocchi. Recipe 33.   *Breaded Fish Sticks.* Buy these at the frozen food counter. Heat in oven with Gnocchi. *Green Pepper Rings.* Parboil pepper rings, brown in oven, use as garnish.

4. *Fish and shellfish, oven style*

This stuffing also may be used with fillets. Just spread over each one, roll up and bake until fish is done.

34   BAKED BASS WITH MUSHROOM STUFFING

Preheat oven to 350° F.
Oven time: about 1 hour   *6-8 servings*

1 4-pound bass
3 tablespoons lemon juice
2 cups day-old bread
½ cup milk
3 tablespoons butter
1 tablespoon minced onion
¼ cup sliced mushrooms
1 tablespoon chopped parsley
1 clove of garlic, mashed
1 egg, slightly beaten
1½ teaspoons salt
¼ teaspoon pepper
Dash of cayenne
Melted butter or oil (for basting fish)

Wash and dry fish inside and out. Remove head and tail. Sprinkle with lemon juice. To make stuffing, soak bread in milk, press out excess. Melt butter in skillet, add onion, mushrooms, parsley and garlic, and cook until onions are soft. Stir in moist bread, remove from heat, then add egg, salt, pepper and cayenne. Fill fish with the stuffing, skewer shut or sew together, brush with melted butter or oil, and bake uncovered in greased shallow baking pan until fish is opaquely white. Baste once or twice with more butter or oil.

FRIDAY FAVORITE

Baked Bass with Mushroom Stuffing. Recipe 34.   *Savory Beets.* Recipe 88.   *Scalloped Cauliflower.* Recipe 91.

For a pretty summer luncheon, set gaily-colored textured place mats as a handsome background for the shells.

35   BAKED STUFFED CLAMS CALIFORNIA

Preheat oven to 400° F.
Oven time: about 20 minutes   *6 servings*

2 cups chopped clams
3 tablespoons butter
2 tablespoons minced onion
¼ cup sliced mushrooms
2 tablespoons minced celery
1 egg, slightly beaten
1 teaspoon salt
Dash of cayenne pepper
Cracker crumbs

Save liquid from chopped clams. Melt butter in skillet, add onion, mushrooms and celery, and cook until tender. Add clam liquid, and cook 5 minutes longer. Remove from heat. Add egg and chopped clams, season to taste with salt, and cayenne, and stir in crumbs to thicken mixture. Turn into 6 large clam shells or individual ramekins, and bake until firm.

36   DEVILED CRABS

Preheat oven to 400° F.
Oven time: 15-20 minutes   *6 servings*

In a saucepan, melt 2 tablespoons butter, stir in 2 tablespoons flour, add 1 cup light cream, 1 teaspoon salt, ½ teaspoon mustard, and ½ teaspoon cayenne pepper. Let cook slowly for 5 minutes, then remove from flame. Gently stir in 2 cups flaked and drained crab meat, ¼ cup soft bread crumbs, and 3 tablespoons grated cheese. Turn into 6 clean crab shells or individual ramekins. Sprinkle with fine crumbs, and bake in oven until tops are delicately brown.

From a Chinese proverb: Cook a fish as you would govern a nation—do not overdo it.

37   ROLLED FLOUNDER FILLETS

Preheat oven to 400° F.
Oven time: about 20 minutes   *6 servings*

6 flounder fillets (about 2 pounds)
2 tablespoons lemon juice
1 teaspoon salt
Dash of cayenne pepper
3 tablespoons grated onion
6 small cooked carrots
6 tablespoons melted butter

Wipe fillets. Sprinkle with lemon juice, salt and cayenne. Spoon half a tablespoon of grated onion over each, top with a carrot. Roll up and secure with a toothpick. Arrange in a greased shallow baking pan, brush with butter, and bake uncovered until fish is firm but still moist. Baste several times with butter.

38   FILLET OF FLOUNDER WITH GRAPES

Preheat oven to 375° F.
Oven time: 20-25 minutes   *6 servings*

Arrange 2 pounds flounder fillets in buttered baking pan, 10" x 6" x 2". Combine 1 grated onion, mashed clove of garlic, 3 tablespoons white wine, salt and pepper, and pour over fish. Refrigerate for several hours. Pour in 1 cup light cream, cover, and bake until fish is tender, and flesh is no longer translucent. Meanwhile, pour boiling water over 1 cup seedless grapes, peel off skins, and drain. Serve fish on heated platter. Spoon sauce from pan over it. Arrange grapes as border.

39   CELERY-SALMON SCALLOP

Preheat oven to 375° F.
Oven time: 30-40 minutes   *6 servings*

2 cups seasoned mashed potatoes
1 egg, slightly beaten
1 1-pound can (2 cups) salmon, flaked
4 tablespoons butter
3 tablespoons minced onion
2 tablespoons minced green pepper
3 tablespoons minced celery
½ cup scalded milk
1 teaspoon lemon juice
½ teaspoon salt
Buttered bread crumbs

Beat potatoes and egg until soft and fluffy, line greased 1½-quart casserole with the mixture. Drain salmon, saving liquid but discarding skin. Melt butter in skillet, add onion, green pepper and celery, and cook until onion is soft. With a fork, gently toss with salmon, milk and lemon juice. Turn into casserole, top with buttered bread crumbs, and bake uncovered, until top is lightly brown. Serve with Celery Pimento Sauce.

CELERY-PIMENTO SAUCE: Add liquid drained from salmon to 1 can condensed cream of celery soup and ¼ cup milk. Heat. Add 3 tablespoons shredded pimentos. Serve in a separate sauceboat.

SUMMER DINNER

Iced Tomato Juice.   Celery-Salmon Scallop. Recipe 39. *Baked Potatoes.* Put into cold oven so they get a head start.   *Salad of Crisp Raw Vegetables.* Mounds of shredded beets, carrots, unpeeled thin-sliced cucumbers, cauliflowerettes.   *French Dressing.*

Use your prettiest casseroles for fish, send them to the table right from your oven.

40   GOLDEN-BROWN SCALLOPS IN BUTTER

Preheat oven to 350° F.
Oven time: 35-45 minutes   *4-6 servings*

1½ pounds bay scallops
1 egg, slightly beaten
2 tablespoons cold water
1 cup fine bread crumbs
1 teaspoon salt
¼ teaspoon pepper
6 tablespoons melted butter or margarine

Wash and dry scallops. Combine egg and water and dip scallops in combination. Season bread crumbs with salt and pepper. Roll scallops in crumbs, put into greased shallow baking dish, and re- frigerate for about half an hour to set coating. Just before baking, pour melted butter or margarine over scallops, put into hot oven until golden brown. Bring to table in oven dish (if you used a pretty one).

41   OVEN-FRIED OYSTERS IN SHELL

Follow recipe above, but arrange the coated oysters in shells instead of baking dish. Bake until oysters are plump, about 20 minutes.

PORCH LUNCHEON

Golden-Brown Scallops in Butter. Recipe 40.   *Cab- bage Polonaise.* Recipe 90. Put into oven with scallops. *Baked Corn on Cob.* Recipe 94. Add corn 20 minutes after fish.   *Melba Toast.* Put thin slices of bread on inverted vegetable dish cover if there is no space on rack.   *Beverage.*

Like folk arts, the best jambalayas are half spontaneous addi-tion, half tradition. Don't be too exact about ingredients, and develop your own jambalayas.

42   SHRIMP AND OYSTER JAMBALAYA

Preheat oven to 375° F.
Oven time: about 1 hour   *4 servings*

1 cup raw rice
1 cup (½ pound) bay scallops
2 cups (about 1 dozen) oysters, drained
3 tablespoons butter or oil
1 medium onion, minced
1 green pepper, minced
2 cloves garlic
1 cup canned tomatoes
2 cups chicken stock, or 2 bouillon cubes dissolved in hot
     water
Salt and pepper

Put rice into greased 2-quart casserole. Add layers of scallops and oysters. Heat butter or oil in skillet, add onion, green pepper, and garlic, and cook until onions are tender. Discard garlic, transfer onion-pepper mixture to casserole, combine canned tomatoes and chicken stock and pour into casserole. Season to taste with salt and pepper. Cover. Bake until rice is done, jambalaya quite moist.

COMPANY'S COMING FOR A FUN MEAL

Shrimp and Oyster Jambalaya. Recipe 42.   *Salad of Grapes, Sliced Oranges, Grapefruit Sections.   Upside-Down Pineapple Cake.* Recipe 131. Put into oven with jambalaya. Serve warm as dessert.   *Beverage.*

Open oysters carefully, combine liquid drained from them with chicken stock to make 1½ cups.

43   OYSTER CASSEROLE AND SPAGHETTINI

Preheat oven to 375° F.
Oven time: about 15 minutes   *4 servings*

½ pound thin spaghetti
4 tablespoons butter or oil
1 small onion, minced
4 tablespoons flour
1½ cups chicken stock
2 tablespoons chopped parsley
4 anchovies, minced
1 teaspoon minced capers
1 teaspoon lemon juice
12 large oysters, cleaned and drained

Cook spaghetti in plenty of boiling water until tender. Drain. Meanwhile combine butter and onion in saucepan, and cook until soft. Stir in flour, chicken stock and parsley. Cook about 15 minutes. Blend in anchovies, capers and lemon juice, and continue cooking a few minutes longer. Fill a greased 2½-quart casserole with alternate layers of spaghetti, oysters, and sauce. Cover and bake until oysters are plump.

OVEN TREAT IN HALF AN HOUR

Oyster Casserole and Spaghettini. Recipe 43.   *Creole Tomatoes.* Recipe 117.   *Potato Puffs.* Buy frozen, bake in oven with tomatoes.   *Vanilla Ice Cream with Toasted Coconut.* Toast shredded coconut in oven with rest of meal. Serve over vanilla ice cream.

Here are two quickies—preheat the oven before you take off your coat to save time when you're late.

44   QUICK TUNA AND MUSHROOM CASSEROLE

Preheat oven to 400° F.
Oven time: about 20 minutes   *4 servings*

1 can (10 ounces) condensed cream of mushroom soup
½ cup light cream
1 can (7 ounces) tuna fish, coarsely flaked and drained
1 teaspoon grated onion
½ teaspoon chopped parsley
½ teaspoon mustard
1 teaspoon salt
½ cup grated American cheese
Potato-chip crumbs

In a 1-quart casserole, mix cream of mushroom soup with cream, add tuna fish, grated onion, parsley, mustard, salt and cheese. Sprinkle top with potato-chip crumbs. Bake in oven until hot and bubbling.

45   FILLETS IN ALMOND SAUCE

Preheat oven to 375° F.
Oven time: about 20 minutes   *4-6 servings*

2 pounds fish fillets
Salt and pepper
1 cup melted butter
½ cup chopped almonds
¼ cup chopped pitted green olives
3 tablespoons white wine

Wipe fillets, dry and arrange them in buttered shallow baking pan. Sprinkle with salt and pepper. Combine other ingredients, and pour over fish. Bake in oven until done.

5. Beef, lamb, and pork—roasts and casseroles

A basic recipe for a tender cut of beef. Do not add water.
Do not cover pan. Add 30 minutes for cold-oven start.

46   ROAST BEEF

Preheat oven to 350° F. for roasts less than 5 pounds
Preheat oven to 325° F. for more than 5 pounds
½ to 1 pound for each serving

Select a tender roast of prime or choice quality. If you are using a meat thermometer, insert it in thickest part of meat where it will not rest on bone. Try to insert thermometer so it will be visible through glass cover. Rest the beef on its bones, or on a rack in the roaster meat pan. Very large roasts may be placed directly on the wire rack in the cooking well. If roast is very lean, brush with oil. This forms a wall that locks in juices.

Cut	Minutes per pound	Internal temperature
STANDING RIBS		
Rare	18-20	140° F.
Medium	22-25	160° F.
Well-Done	27-30	170° F.
ROLLED RIBS		
Rare	30-35	140° F.
Medium	35-40	160° F.
Well-Done	40-45	170° F.
PRIME QUALITY RUMP		
Medium	35-40	160° F.
Well-Done	40-45	170° F.
SIRLOIN TIP		
Rare	20-25	140° F.
Medium	30-35	160° F.
Well-Done	35-40	170° F.

Of course you want gravy with pot roast. Make it from the drippings as you usually do.

47   QUICK POT ROAST

Preheat oven to 350° F.   *¾-1 pound per serving*

Tough cuts of beef cannot be roasted by dry heat. Brown beef, chopped onions, tomatoes, celery, under broiler, in hot fat in saucepan, or in oven preheated to 500° F. Place in roaster meat pan, and add ½ cup water. Bake until tender. One hour before it is done, you may surround beef with partly-cooked potatoes, carrots, or other vegetables. (Raw vegetables take twice as long, lose food value and flavor in the process.)

Cuts	*Total Oven Time*
¾-inch thick	About 1 hour
1-inch thick	1¼ to 1½ hours
1½-inches thick	1½ to 2 hours
2-inches thick	2 to 3 hours
large pot roasts	3 to 4 hours

48   JUICY SLOW POT ROAST

Start in cold oven
Set temperature at 250° F.
Oven time: 3-3½ hours   *6-8 servings*

Season a 4-pound pot roast generously with salt and pepper. For marinade sauce combine 1 cup olive oil, 1 cup white or red wine, 1 mashed clove of garlic, 2 tablespoons finely-chopped celery, 1 tablespoon finely-chopped parsley, 2 teaspoons chopped basil leaves. Pour over roast, and let stand at least 6 hours, turning 3 or 4 times. Drain (save marinade), and wipe dry. Brown as above. Transfer browned meat and marinade to roaster pan. Bake until done as you like it. Test with fork for doneness after 3 hours. Serve with pan juices. Slow heat makes this roast tender and good.

49   CARAWAY SWISS STEAK WITH ROAST POTATOES

Preheat oven to 325° F.
Oven time: 1½ hours   *4-6 servings*

2 pounds round or rump steak, cut 1-inch thick
3 tablespoons flour
3 tablespoons fat or oil
1 onion, chopped
1 cup tomato sauce
1 bay leaf
1 mashed clove of garlic
1 tablespoon caraway seeds
1½ teaspoons salt
¼ teaspoon pepper
6 medium potatoes, partly cooked

Wipe steak, then pound in flour. Heat fat or oil, and brown steak. (Steak may also be browned under broiler, set as close to heat as possible.) Transfer to meat pan. Top with onion. Combine tomato sauce, bay leaf, garlic, caraway seeds, salt and pepper. Spoon over steak. Bake for 45 minutes, then surround meat with potatoes (which have been cooked for no more than 8-10 minutes in boiling salted water, then drained). Spoon some of the pan juices around potatoes, so they brown evenly. Continue baking until meat is almost tender enough to eat with a spoon. If pan seems to be getting too dry, add hot beef stock or tomato sauce. Remove bay leaf and garlic, if you can find it, before serving.

WINTER FAMILY SUPPER

Caraway Swiss Steak with Roast Potatoes. Recipe 49.
Carrot Ring with Buttered Peas. Recipe 92. Add carrots half an hour after roast. Fill with peas just before serving.
Apricot Fluff. Recipt 142. Put into oven with carrots. Serve warm as dessert.   *Hot Tea or Coffee.*

50   MEAT PIE PARMIGIANA

Preheat oven to 375° F.
Oven time: about 1 hour   *4 servings*

3 slices white bread
¼ cup milk
½ pound chopped beef
½ pound chopped veal
1 egg, slightly beaten
1 medium onion, grated
1 teaspoon salt
¼ teaspoon pepper
2 cups seasoned mashed potatoes
½ cup grated Parmesan cheese

Soak bread in milk, then squeeze out excess liquid. Combine bread with beef, veal, egg, onion, ½ cup water, salt and pepper. Blend well. Spread half the mixture into a greased 1½-quart casserole, add a layer of mashed potatoes and cheese; repeat layers, ending with cheese. Bake uncovered until brown.

51   OLD-FASHIONED COUNTRY LOAF

Preheat oven to 375° F.
Oven time: about 1 hour   *6 servings*

Mix together 2 pounds ground beef, ¾ cup finely-chopped onions, ¼ cup finely-chopped green pepper, salt and pepper to taste. Combine with 1 cup finely-crushed corn flakes, and 2 slightly-beaten eggs. Shape into loaf, place in greased meat pan, or, for a crusty loaf, bake in a shallow baking pan. A loaf pan 8″ x 4″ x 3½″ is fine. Serve with tomato sauce made by heating undiluted cream of tomato soup with drippings from loaf.

GO-TOGETHERS

Meat Pie Parmigiani. Recipe 50.   *Baked Deviled Tomatoes.* Recipe 116.   *Pineapple Brown Betty.* Recipe 149. Serve extras tomorrow.

52   ITALIAN BEEF ROLLS WITH SHELL MACARONI

Preheat oven to 350° F.
Oven time: about 30 minutes   *8 servings*

2 tablespoons olive oil
2 cloves of garlic, mashed
2 pounds minute steaks (thin beefsteaks scored at the market)
½ pound ground pork
1 cup water
1 No. 2½ can Italian tomatoes
1 6-ounce can Italian tomato paste
1 teaspoon salt
1 teaspoon sugar
½ teaspoon oregano
¼ teaspoon red pepper
6 cups cooked shell macaroni

Heat oil in large skillet. Add garlic and minute steaks. Brown them on both sides, then transfer to a platter. In same skillet, add pork and let it brown on all sides. Add water, tomatoes, tomato paste, salt, sugar, oregano and pepper. Bring to quick boil. Cook for about 15 minutes. Roll up minute steaks and place in layers in a deep casserole. Pour the sauce over them. Cover, and bake until beef is tender, and the sauce thick. Serve over cooked shell macaroni.

SAVORY OVEN MEAL

Italian Beef Rolls with Shell Macaroni. Recipe 52.   *Glazed Onions.* Recipe 99.   *Baked Pears.* Cut 4 firm pears in half. Put into greased baking dish. Combine ½ cup brown sugar, ½ cup granulated sugar, 3 tablespoons butter, 1 teaspoon grated lemon rind. Sprinkle over pears. Put ¾ cup water into baking dish. Bake with beef rolls. Whip 3 ounces soft cream cheese with milk until fluffy. Pile into pear hollows. Serve as dessert.

One of these zesty-flavored dishes for which the Italian cuisine is famous.

Most everyone likes these well-seasoned loaves.

53   INDIVIDUAL BEEF AND LIVER LOAVES

Preheat oven to 400° F.
Oven time: 40-50 minutes   *6-8 servings*

1½ pounds beef
½ pound beef liver
3 tablespoons bacon drippings or other fat
¼ cup chopped onions
3 tablespoons flour
1 can condensed cream of mushroom soup
1 cup soft bread crumbs
Salt and pepper

Remove gristle from beef. Remove tubes and membranes from liver. Grind, using fine blade. Heat fat in skillet, brown onions. Stir in flour, add soup and bring to a quick boil. Combine with ground meat, crumbs, salt and pepper to taste. Shape into 6 oval loaves, arrange in greased shallow pan, and bake until brown.

EMPHASIS ON ECONOMY

How to manage: Bake loaves and beets. Make peach cobbler and put into oven 20 minutes after loaves.
Individual Beef and Liver Loaves. Recipe 53.   *Savory Beets.* Recipe 88.   *Peach Cobbler.* In saucepan, bring to boil 2 cups thin-sliced peaches, ½ cup sugar, ¼ cup water, 2 tablespoons orange juice. Meanwhile beat 1 egg, ½ cup sugar, 2 tablespoons butter or shortening. Add 1 tablespoon milk, stir in ½ cup all-purpose flour, ½ teaspoon baking powder, ¼ teaspoon salt. Spread batter into greased 8″ x 8″ x 2″ baking pan. Cover with peaches from saucepan. Bake 25-35 minutes. Serve warm.

54   CARBONADO

Preheat oven to 325° F.
Oven time: about 1¼ hours   *6 servings*

1½ cups dried apricots
1½ cups dried pears
4 tablespoons oil
¼ cup diced onions
1 medium tomato, diced
2 pounds ground beef
2 cups diced potatoes
1 cup diced celery
1 cup diced carrots
1¼ teaspoons salt
¼ teaspoon pepper
1 cup beef stock or 1 bouillon cube dissolved in hot water
½ cup seedless raisins
Note: Keep adding more beef stock or hot water as necessary.
1 teaspoon salt

Soak apricots and pears in water to soften. Heat oil in skillet, add onions, tomato and beef, and brown very lightly—just enough so that beef loses its bright red color. Transfer to greased 2½-quart casserole or roaster meat pan. Drain apricots and pears, and arrange around beef, then add celery, carrots, salt and pepper, pour in beef stock. Cover and bake until fruit is tender and liquid almost evaporated. When done, drop in the raisins, and stir to blend with the rest of the stew. Serve this fragrant casserole with hot cooked rice.

LATIN-AMERICAN STYLE

Note: If casserole seems to be drying out, add more hot water or beef stock as necessary.
Carbonado. Recipe 54.   *Stuffed Green Peppers.* Recipe 101. Bake for last 25 minutes.   *Tomato, Scallion and Olive Salad.*

There are as many variations of Musaca as there are Romanians. Here is one way it is done.

55   MUSACA, A ROMANIAN CASSEROLE

Preheat oven to 350° F.
Oven time: about 1 hour   *6 servings*

3 tablespoons oil or lard
1 small onion, diced
1 eggplant, diced
1 clove of garlic, mashed
1½ pounds ground beef
1 teaspoon salt
¼ teaspoon pepper
Dash of paprika
1 cup chopped tomatoes

Heat oil or lard in large skillet. Add onion, eggplant, and garlic, and let them brown. Discard garlic, transfer browned vegetables to casserole. Combine ground beef, salt, pepper and paprika, and brown in same skillet. In a greased 2-quart casserole, arrange layers of eggplant-onion mixture and browned beef. Heat tomatoes in skillet. Pour into casserole. Cover, and bake until beef is done. Check once or twice, and if it shows signs of drying out, add boiling beef stock or water. Serve with Rice-Filled Green Peppers.

FOR LARGE LUNCHEON APPETITES

Musaca. Recipe 55.   *Buttermilk Corn Meal Rolls.* Recipe 122. Bake these first. Remove from oven and bake remainder of meal.   *Potatoes Royale with Swiss Cheese.* Recipe 106.

For color, top this casserole with cooked green pepper strips, or green peas.

56   CALF'S LIVER CASSEROLE

Preheat oven to 350° F.
Oven time: about 1 hour   *4-6 servings*

6 carrots, quartered lengthwise
3 large turnips, cut into thick slices
3 small white onions
3 beets, cut into thick rounds
2 pounds calf's liver, cut into long strips
2 tablespoons butter
2 tablespoons flour
Salt and pepper

Cook carrots, turnips and onions in boiling, salted water for 12 minutes. (They should be only partially cooked.) Save 1 cup liquid for later use. Cook beets in separate saucepan. In greased roaster meat pan or casserole, arrange layers of food as follows: beets, liver, carrots, liver, turnips, liver and onions. Make white sauce: Melt butter in saucepan, stir in flour, add 1 cup liquid drained from vegetables. Season to taste. Cook until thick. Pour into casserole, bake uncovered until vegetables and liver are tender.

UNUSUAL COMBINATIONS

How to manage: Bake biscuits first. Reduce oven heat, bake remainder of meal.
Calf's Liver Casserole. Recipe 56. Top with green pepper strips.   *Baked Sweet Potatoes.* Scrub them. Bake on rack alongside casserole. Press out pulp to remove steam before serving.   *Bacon Biscuits.* Recipe 125.

Do not substitute calves' liver. Its more delicate flavor requires subtle handling, and a barbecue sauce is anything but subtle.

57   TANGY BARBECUED LIVER

Preheat oven to 350° F.
Oven time: 30-40 minutes   *4 servings*

1 pound beef liver, cut into slices ½-inch thick
3 tablespoons olive oil
1 large onion, sliced thin
1 teaspoon sugar
⅛ teaspoon pepper
¼ teaspoon salt
6 tablespoons catsup
¼ cup vinegar
¼ cup water
1 tablespoon Worcestershire sauce
Dash of Tabasco sauce

Wipe liver with damp cloth, and remove skin and tubes. Brown in hot oil in skillet. Arrange in greased casserole, or shallow baking dish. In same skillet, adding more oil if necessary, brown onions. Pour in other ingredients, let cook for 10 minutes, then turn onto liver. Cover, and place in hot oven. Bake until liver is tender. Uncover for last 15 minutes if there is too much liquid, and bake until reduced.

IT'S A BARBECUE

How to manage: Bake cake first; reduce oven temperature and continue with remainder of meal.
Tangy Barbecued Liver. Recipe 57.   *Pimentoes Ranchero.* Recipe 100. Bake at 350°.   *Onion and Apple Casserole.* Recipe 98. Cut onions and apples very thin so they are done at same time as liver.   *Quick Chocolate Cake.* Recipe 130.   *Cold Milk or Iced Coffee.*

When loaf is done, cool, remove from pan, and cut into serving slices.

58   VEAL LOAF AND VEGETABLE CASSEROLE

Preheat oven to 350° F.
Oven time: about 1½ hours   *6 servings*

1¾ cups milk
4 medium potatoes
6 small white onions
6 small carrots
4 tablespoons butter
4 tablespoons flour
1 cup milk
1 teaspoon salt
⅛ teaspoon pepper
1½ pounds ground veal (breast, shoulder or round)

Heat milk in a saucepan, add vegetables, cover and cook until barely tender. Drain. Save the milk. Melt butter, stir in flour, then add milk (about 1-1¼ cups), drained from vegetables, and salt and pepper. Cook for a few minutes until thickened. Pour into the veal. Mash potatoes, mix well with veal, then shape into loaf. Place in deep oval baking dish, surround with cooked onions and carrots, sprinkle with paprika, and bake until loaf is firm. This makes a moist loaf.

WINTER DELIGHT

Veal Loaf and Vegetable Casserole. Recipe 58.   *Baked Winter Squash Filled with Stewed Tomatoes.* Recipe 115. *Hot Bread.* Warm it in oven.   *Rhubarb and Pineapple Meringue.* Recipe 150. Bake for last 20 minutes. Serve warm as dessert.

You can vary this recipe by adding claret or Marsala wine to replace part of mushroom liquid.

59   VEAL MARENGO

Preheat oven to 350° F.
Oven time: about 1¼ hours   *4-6 servings*

2 pounds veal (leg, shoulder, or breast)
2 tablespoons bacon fat
2 medium onions, chopped
1 clove of garlic
¼ cup sliced mushrooms, fresh or canned
1 cup mushroom liquid or water
2 tablespoons Italian tomato paste
1 tablespoon soy sauce

Cut veal into 1½-inch squares. Heat bacon fat in flameproof baking dish. Add veal and brown on both sides. Transfer to platter. Brown onions, garlic and mushrooms in same baking dish. Add mushroom liquid or water, tomato paste and soy sauce. Bring to quick boil. Put browned veal back into baking dish, cover and bake in hot oven until veal is tender and sauce has been reduced to about half. This dish is not harmed by overcooking, but check from time to time to be sure that sauce has not evaporated. Add hot water, a little at a time, if necessary.

GOURMET SUPPER

Veal Marengo. Recipe 59.   *Eggplant Soufflé.* Recipe 95.
   Club Potatoes. Recipe 103.   *Garlic Toasted Bread Sticks.* Buy Italian breadsticks, roll in melted butter combined with mashed garlic. Heat in oven for 15 minutes.
Oven Compote of Fruit. Recipt 152. Reduce amounts.

If you like lamb slightly rare in the French manner, use minimum times and internal temperatures.

60   ROAST LAMB IN PINEAPPLE MARINADE

Preheat oven to 325° F.
Oven time: see chart below   *½ pound per serving*

6-7 pound leg of lamb
1 cup unsweetened pineapple juice
¼ cup oil
3 tablespoons chopped onion
1 clove of garlic, mashed
1 tablespoon celery seed
3 tablespoons lemon juice

Trim surplus fat from meat, but do not remove fell (thin paper skin). Combine other ingredients, and pour over lamb in deep bowl. Refrigerate for at least 4 hours, or as long as 24, turning 3 or 4 times. Transfer lamb to roasting pan with the marinade, and roast until done.

	Weight	Oven temperature	Thermometer temperature	Minutes per pound
LEG OF LAMB	Up to 6 pounds	325° F.	175°-180° F.	35-40
"	Over 6 pounds	325° F.	175°-180° F.	30-35
BONED & ROLLED	3-5 pounds	325° F.	175°-180° F.	45
"	5 or more	325° F.	175°-180° F.	40
CUSHION	3-4	325° F.	175°-180° F.	40-45
ROLLED SHOULDER	3-4	325° F.	175°-180° F.	40-45

NOTES ABOUT LAMB

The delicate texture and relatively low juiciness of lamb requires slow, even cooking. Your roaster-oven with its exact temperature dial brings out the best in the meat. Serve it either hot or cold. Lamb fat has a high melting point and becomes pasty when lukewarm.

61   LAMB RAGOUT WITH PIMENTO BISCUITS

Preheat oven to 425° F.
Oven time: about 15 minutes   *6 servings*

1 can condensed cream of mushroom soup
¼ cup milk
½ teaspoon Worcestershire sauce
2 cups cooked diced lamb
12 tiny cooked white onions
1½ cups cooked diced potatoes
1 partly-cooked green pepper, cut into rings
1 cup sifted all-purpose flour
1½ teaspoons baking powder
½ teaspoon salt
3 tablespoons shortening
⅓ cup milk
¼ cup finely chopped pimentos

Heat soup and milk to simmering. Remove from flame. Add Worcestershire and gently blend with lamb, onions, and potatoes. Turn into greased 2½-quart casserole. Top with green pepper rings. Make baking powder biscuits: Sift together flour, baking powder, and salt. Cut in shortening. Stir in milk to make dough. Roll out ¼-inch thick on floured board. Sprinkle with pimentos. Roll as you would a jelly roll. Cut into slices ¾ inch thick. Place on lamb in casserole, and bake uncovered until brown. (About 12 biscuits.)

DINNER FOR OLD FRIENDS

Bacon-Wrapped Cauliflowerets. Recipe 2. Bake while oven is preheating. *Toasted Almonds.   Cocktails.   Lamb Ragout with Pimento Biscuits.* Recipe 61.   *Apple Slices Baked with Honey.* Curried Tomatoes. Season firm tomatoes with salt, pepper, butter, curry powder. Bake.   *Hot French Rolls.   Fresh Fruit Salad.   Coffee.*

62   NEW ORLEANS LAMB AND BEAN CASSEROLE

Preheat oven to 375° F.
Oven time: about 1 hour   *6-8 servings*

1½ cups dried navy beans
6-8 thin shoulder lamb chops
3 tablespoons olive oil
1 cup chopped onions
1 clove of garlic, mashed
Salt and pepper
½ teaspoon chopped wild marjoram
1 tablespoon butter
1 cup chicken stock, or 1 chicken bouillon cube dissolved
    in hot water

Soak beans overnight in water to cover. Next day, cook them until barely tender. Brown chops in hot skillet, turning once so both sides are seared. Set aside. Heat oil in skillet, add onions, garlic, salt, pepper and marjoram. Cook until onions are soft. Discard garlic. In casserole, arrange a layer of beans, a layer of chops, and a layer of onions. Melt butter in chicken stock and pour into casserole. Cover; bake until chops are tender.

FEATURING LAMB CHOPS

How to manage: Do lamb and beans, onions and apples first, but increase oven temperature for last 15 minutes, add biscuits. Check lamb casserole to be sure it has enough liquid.
New Orleans Lamb and Bean Casserole. Recipe 62.   *Onion and Apple Casserole.* Recipe 98.   *Parsley Biscuits.* Recipe 125.

CHINESE-STYLE MENU: *Chinese Roast Pork, Oven Baked Rice* (Recipe 8) *with Cooked Chopped Shrimp, bought Almond Cakes* or Cookies (Recipe 133).

63   CHINESE ROAST PORK

Start in cold oven set at 350° F.
Oven time: about 1 hour   *6 servings*

2 pounds pork loin, butt or shoulder
3 tablespoons soy sauce
1 tablespoon sherry wine
1 tablespoon sugar
1 teaspoon salt
¼ teaspoon pepper
1 clove of garlic, peeled and mashed
1 small piece fresh ginger, mashed

Cut pork with the grain into strips 2 inches wide. Combine other ingredients and pour over strips. Refrigerate for one or two hours. Put on rack in shallow baking pan, and bake until tender and thoroughly cooked. Slice each strip, against the grain this time, and serve with mustard sauce, or dry mustard thinned with water.

Mustard Sauce: Combine ¼ cup prepared mustard, 1 tablespoon soy sauce, and dash of turmeric. Mix well.

64   SUCCULENT PORK ROAST WITH BRUSSELS SPROUTS

Preheat oven to 350° F.
Oven time: about 40 minutes per pound

Select fresh ham, shoulder or center loin pork roast. Wipe. Rub with cut clove of garlic. Season with salt, pepper and sage. Insert meat thermometer in thickest part of roast, not resting on bone. Place meat on rack in shallow pan, and put in oven. Roast to internal temperature of 185° F., or until no trace of pink is left in meat. Forty minutes before roast is done, surround it with half-cooked Brussels sprouts topped with grated onion.

65   STUFFED PORK TENDERLOIN

Start in cold oven
Oven time: 1¼ hours   *6 servings*

3 pork tenderloins (about ¾ pound each)
2 tablespoons butter
¼ cup minced onion
1 cup soft bread crumbs
¼ teaspoon salt
⅛ teaspoon pepper
6 slices bacon

Have tenderloins cut lengthwise almost through to the bottom. Melt butter in a saucepan, and cook onion until tender but not brown. Add other ingredients. Blend with a fork. Stuff tenderloins with this mixture, skewer edges or tie them together with a string, and put on a rack in a shallow pan. Put bacon slices over them, and roast until well done. Remove skewers before serving.

66   PERFECT BAKED BACON

Start in cold oven set at 400° F.
Oven time: 15-20 minutes

Place unseparated strips of bacon on a rack in a shallow pan, overlapping so that the fat edge of one slice is on the lean edge of the next. Bake until bacon is as crisp as you like it. No turning, no draining, no curling.

FOR CRISPER BACON

Arrange slices *not* overlapping on rack in shallow pan. Bake until done as you like.

Do not overcook spaghetti. It should be al dente—*soft but not spineless.*

67   PORK CHOP, APPLE AND SPAGHETTI CASSEROLE

Preheat oven to 350° F.
Oven time: about 1 hour   *6 servings*

8 ounces spaghetti, cooked *al dente*
6 pork chops
¼ cup chopped onions
2 cups pared, cored, and cubed apples
2 tablespoons brown sugar
1 teaspoon salt
¼ teaspoon pepper

Arrange cooked spaghetti in bottom of greased casserole pretty enough to carry to the table. Brown chops in skillet, turn to brown both sides, then transfer to casserole. In same skillet, cook onions and apples in ½ cup water for 10 minutes. Put over chops, sprinkle with brown sugar, salt, and pepper, cover and bake until chops are tender. This may also be baked starting in a cold oven. If so, add 20 minutes to total baking time.

ONE HOUR OVEN MEAL

How to manage: Bake soufflé when rest of oven meal is done. *Pork Chop, Apple and Spaghetti Casserole.* Recipe 67. *Cabbage Polonaise.* Recipe 90. Bake at 350° for 1 hour. *Baked Mushrooms.* Spread out 1½ pounds sliced mushrooms in shallow baking dish. Season with 2 teaspoons salt, dash of pepper. Dot generously with butter. Add ½ cup beef stock and 2 tablespoons wine. Cover and bake ½ hour.   *Banana Soufflé.* Recipe 145, but add 3 tablespoons powdered sugar and 2 tablespoons butter to mashed pulp. Serve with whipped cream.

68   CURRIED APRICOT PORK CHOPS

Preheat oven to 350° F.
Oven time: about 1 hour   *6 servings*

6 pork chops
2 tablespoons butter
2 tablespoons flour
2 teaspoons curry powder
Dash of salt
1 cup undiluted evaporated milk
¼ cup mushroom stems or pieces
4 tablespoons canned tomato sauce
¼ cup raisins
2 tablespoons apricot sirup
6 canned apricots, pitted

Brown chops on both sides in hot skillet. Pour off excess fat, and transfer chops to roaster meat pan. In same skillet, melt butter, add flour, curry powder, and salt. Gradually stir in milk until sauce is smooth. Add mushrooms, tomato sauce, raisins, and sirup, and pour over chops. Place apricots around chops, not touching sides of pan. Bake until chops are tender.

69   PORK CHOPS AND VEGETABLES IN SOUR CREAM

Preheat oven to 350° F.
Oven time: about 1 hour   *4 servings*

Brown 4 thick pork chops on all sides in hot skillet; transfer to casserole. In same skillet (adding oil if necessary), brown ½ cup chopped onions and 1 cup sliced mushrooms. Spoon over chops, and add 1 package (defrosted) frozen lima beans. Season with salt and pepper to taste. Pour in ¼ cup hot water. Cover and bake until chops are tender, then add 1½ cups sour cream. Continue baking for 10 minutes until done.

This is a basic recipe. However, since ham is packed in many different ways, follow wrapper directions when given.

70   BAKED GLAZED HAM

Preheat oven to 325° F.
Oven time: see chart   *½ pound per serving*

1 whole smoked cook-before-serving ham
1 cup brown sugar
½ cup peach or pineapple preserves

Place ham, fat side up, on rack in shallow roasting pan. Insert meat thermometer into center of thickest part, not touching bone. Bake uncovered, without water. Half an hour before end of baking time, take ham from oven. Spoon out drippings. Remove rind with sharp knife. To score, cut entire fat surface into squares or diamonds. (Stick cord into fat with toothpicks to serve as guide for even lines). Combine sugar with preserves (or use honey, corn sirup, or your favorite glaze), put ham back into oven, and continue baking until lustrous and golden. For easier carving, allow ham to stand at least 15 minutes. For ready-to-eat fully-cooked hams, cut baking times in half. Bake to internal temperature of 160° F.

Weight of Bone-in Uncooked Ham	*Total Oven Time*
5-8 pounds	2¾-3½ hours
8-10 pounds	3½-3¾ hours
10-14 pounds	3¾-4¼ hours
14-22 pounds	4¼-5¾ hours

Weight of Boneless Uncooked ham	*Total oven time*
4-8 pounds	2½-3½ hours
8-12 pounds	3½-4 hours
12-14 pounds	4-4½ hours

Ancient Chinese cook say ham and pineapple make happy stomach. Modern gourmet say cheese toast make it ecstatic. Try this good combination for lunch.

71   PINEAPPLE HAM ROLLS WITH CHEESE TOAST

Preheat oven to 400° F.
Oven time: about 30 minutes   *4 servings*

3 tablespoons pineapple sirup
1 tablespoon prepared mustard
8 thin slices cooked ham
8 pineapple sticks (these come in cans)
4 slices white bread
Butter
4 slices Gruyére cheese
Freshly-grated pepper

Combine sirup and mustard and spread over ham. Place a pineapple stick in each slice; roll up and secure with toothpicks. Arrange in greased shallow baking dish. Cover and bake. Meanwhile toast bread, cut slices in half diagonally, spread with cheese, and put into oven until cheese melts (about 15 minutes). Grate pepper over cheese, and serve immediately with thoroughly heated ham rolls. Allow 2 for each serving.

PRETTY LUNCHEON FOR THE CLUB

How to manage: Arrange bananas in shallow baking dish pretty enough to go to the table. Spread them out with points meeting in center. Arrange apricots between banana spokes.
Pineapple Ham Rolls with Cheese Toast. Recipe 71.
Baked Bananas. Recipe 144.   *Filled Apricots.* Fill canned pitted apricots with cooked rice. Dry. Roll in butter and brown sugar. Bake uncovered until brown.

*Try these spareribs for a Saturday night company snack
. . . this is finger fare and conducive to informality.*

72   BARBECUED SPARERIBS IN PIQUANT SAUCE

Preheat oven to 450° F.
Reduce to 350° F.
Oven time: about 1¼ hours   *4-6 servings*

3 pounds spareribs
2 cloves garlic
¾ cup chili sauce
½ cup orange marmalade
¼ cup soy sauce

Have spareribs cut into 4-inch sections. Rub them well with
garlic. Arrange in greased roaster meat pan. Sear in oven on both
sides (allow about 20 minutes). Do not cover pan. Meanwhile
mix chili sauce, marmalade, and soy sauce. As soon as spareribs
are seared, spoon half the sauce over them. Reduce heat to 350° F.
and bake about 20 minutes longer. Turn ribs, coat with remaining sauce, and continue baking until ribs are well done, crisply
brown. Serve with pan juices.

SPARERIBS IN APPLE JUICE

After arranging spareribs in greased meat pan, as above,
cover them with ½ cup chopped onions. Bake for 20
minutes. Reduce heat to 350°, combine 1 cup apple juice,
3 tablespoons lemon juice, ½ cup catsup, 1 teaspoon prepared mustard, 1 teaspoon salt, and ¼ teaspoon pepper.
Pour over ribs. Continue baking 40 minutes longer. Remove cover for last 10 minutes.

6. Baked chicken and other oven specialties

Don't cover pan, don't add water, don't stuff until ready to roast, don't stuff too full.

73   MARVELOUS ROAST STUFFED TURKEY

Preheat oven to 350° F.
Oven time: about 35 minutes per pound   *6 servings*

1 whole roasting chicken, duck, goose or turkey
    (about 4 pounds ready to cook)
Giblets (heart, gizzard, liver)
1 medium onion
5 slices day-old bread
1 teaspoon marjoram
1 teaspoon dried parsley
Salt and pepper
3 tablespoons melted butter or fat

Wash and dry poultry inside and out. Cook heart, gizzard and liver (added last) until tender. Drain and save liquid. Put giblets and onion through meat grinder, using fine blade. Soak bread in giblet stock, squeeze dry, combine with giblets. Add marjoram, parsley, salt, pepper and mix well. Stuff into neck and body. Skewer or sew openings. Brush with fat; roast on rack in pan. When drumstick (held with paper towel) is tender and rotates easily, the bird is done. Remove, and use drippings in pan to make gravy.

POULTRY ROASTING TIME TABLE

Weight	Oven Temperature	Total time
3-4 pounds	350° F.	2-2½ hours
4-8 pounds	325° F.	2¼-3¼ hours
8-14 pounds	325° F.	3-3½ hours
14-20 pounds	300° F.	3½-4½ hours

This is Judith Hall's recipe for crusty chicken which tastes fried but is baked in the oven.

74   EASY OVEN-FRIED CHICKEN

Preheat oven to 400°-450° F.
Oven time: about 1 hour   *4 servings*

2 quartered broiling chickens, each 2-2½ pounds
    ready to cook
1 egg, slightly beaten
2 tablespoons water
1½ teaspoons salt
½ teaspoon pepper
2 cups corn flakes, rolled fine
8 tablespoons butter or margarine

Clean and wipe chicken. Combine egg and water, salt and pepper. Dip chicken quarters into mixture, then roll in corn flakes. Let dry for a minute or two. Arrange in a greased, shallow 2-quart casserole. Melt butter or margarine (you can do this in an ovenware butter melter while oven is getting hot). Pour over chicken. Bake uncovered until chicken is fork-tender. Baste with butter several times if chicken shows tendency to dry out.

PICNIC IN THE BACKYARD

How to manage: Bake everything in oven preheated to 450°.
Easy Oven-Fried Chicken. Recipe 74.   *Oven "French-Fried" Potatoes.* Recipe 107. Or heat frozen ones for 10-15 minutes.   *Sliced Tomatoes.*   *Buttered Green Beans.*
Buttermilk Biscuits. Recipe 125.   *California Fruit Salad.* Arrange in pretty pattern: small bunches seedless grapes, unpared apple slices, banana chunks, canned pineapple wedges. Serve with French dressing made with orange juice instead of vinegar.   *Tossed Green Salad.*   *Oven Heated Rolls.*   *Oregon Apple Pudding.* Recipe 141. *Iced Tea.*

While your neighbor struggles with charcoal and smoke, just plug your roaster into an electric outlet on the porch and enjoy this meal.

75   BARBECUED BAKED CHICKEN

Preheat oven to 375° F.
Oven time: about 1 hour   *6 servings*

2 cut-up broiling chickens, each about 2½ pounds
    ready to cook
¼ cup water
¼ cup heavy cream
¼ cup butter or oil
3 tablespoons catsup
3 tablespoons lemon juice
2 teaspoons sugar
1 clove garlic, mashed
1 teaspoon salt
¼ teaspoon pepper
¼ teaspoon Tabasco sauce

Clean chickens inside and out. Dry them, then place skin side up in shallow baking dish. Combine water and cream and pour over chicken. Bake uncovered. Meanwhile make barbecue sauce: Mix butter or oil, catsup, lemon juice, sugar, garlic, salt, pepper and Tabasco sauce in an ovenware dish. Let it heat while chicken bakes. After 30 minutes, pour barbecue sauce over chicken and continue baking 30 minutes longer.

OVEN BARBECUE ON A PORCH

Barbecued Baked Chicken
Corn on Cob in Foil. Wrap in foil, bake alongside chicken
    for last 15 minutes.   *Whole Tomatoes.   Hot Rolls.*
    Iced Drinks.

Traditionally made in a shallow casserole in which it is sent to the table. Cooked artichokes are sometimes added.

76   POLLO CON ARROZ

Preheat oven to 375° F.
Oven time: about 1 hour   *6 servings*

1 cup raw rice
2 tablespoons olive oil
1 cut-up roasting chicken, about 5 pounds ready to cook
1 No. 2 can tomatoes
1 green pepper, finely chopped
1 clove of garlic, mashed
1 cup chicken stock, or bouillon cube dissolved in hot water
¼ teaspoon Spanish saffron
Salt and pepper
¼ cup Madeira or sherry wine
1 package frozen peas
3 tablespoons canned shredded pimentos

Brown rice in hot oil in skillet on top of stove, transfer to greased 3-quart casserole. In same skillet, adding more oil, brown chicken on all sides. Transfer to casserole. In skillet, heat tomatoes, green pepper, garlic, chicken stock, saffron, and salt and pepper to taste. As soon as sauce boils, pour over chicken. Add wine, cover casserole, and bake until chicken is tender. During the last few minutes, blend in peas and pimentos and serve when peas are cooked.

DINNER WITH A LATIN-AMERICAN ACCENT

Avocado and Grapefruit Salad. Serve grapefruit sections in avocado halves; French dressing.
Pollo Con Arroz
Orange Coconut Pudding. Recipe 148. Bake it at 375° in oven alongside Pollo Con Arroz. Same temperature, same time. Serve warm.

77   SAVORY STUFFED DRUMSTICKS

Preheat oven to 375° F.
Oven time: about 45 minutes   *8 servings*

8 drumsticks
⅓ cup minced cooked ham
⅓ cup finely-chopped celery
2 tablespoons cracker crumbs
4 tablespoons melted butter
3 cups cooked rice
1 cup canned pineapple chunks
1 cup chicken stock

Simmer drumsticks in boiling salted water until barely tender. Drain, saving the stock. Remove and discard bones. Combine ham, celery, crumbs and 2 tablespoons butter, and use to stuff drumsticks. Transfer to greased 2½-quart casserole or baking dish. Brush with remaining butter. Surround with rice and pineapple chunks. Pour in chicken stock, cover and bake until drumsticks are tender. If there is a great deal of liquid in casserole, remove cover, turn up oven to 425°, and bake until excess liquid evaporates.

PATIO PARTY

How to manage: Start bread in preheated oven 25 minutes before rest of meal.
Savory Stuffed Drumsticks. Recipe 77.   *Creole Tomatoes.* Recipe 117.   *Baked Rice.* Recipe 28. Bake at 375° same time as drumsticks.   *Baked Apples in Maple Sirup.* Recipe 140. Double amounts. Bake in dish on inverted casserole covers.   *Banana Tea Bread.* Recipe 118.

78   COQ AU VIN

Preheat oven to 375° F.
Oven time: about 1 hour   *6 servings*

1 cut-up roasting chicken, 4-5 pounds ready to cook
Salt and pepper
4 tablespoons butter or oil
3 tablespoons brandy
1½ cups Burgundy or claret wine
12 small white onions
6 small carrots, cut lengthwise into quarters
1 clove of garlic, mashed
½ cup sliced mushrooms
1 tablespoon chopped parsley
½ teaspoon rosemary
Dash of cloves

Season chicken with salt and pepper. Heat butter or oil, add chicken, a few pieces at a time, and brown on all sides. Transfer them to a large casserole as they brown. Sprinkle with brandy (warmed in oven that has been preheating) set brandy afire, then douse flame with part of the wine. Surround chicken with onions, carrots, and mushrooms. Combine garlic (mine goes through garlic press, otherwise mash it well), parsley, rosemary, cloves, and remainder of wine. Pour into casserole, cover and bake until chicken is tender when tested with fork. Remove cover for last half hour so sauce cooks down. This is traditionally served with toast fingers, made from sliced white bread browned in oven.

CHICKEN SPECIALTY FOR COMPANY

Cocktails.   Ham and Mushrooms in Pastry Shells. Recipe 4. Cut amounts in half.   *Coq Au Vin.* Recipe 78. *Cooked Buttered Noodles.   Toast Fingers.   Cucumber Boats.* Scoop out meat from slender unpared cucumbers sliced lengthwise in half. Marinate with thin radish slices, minced anchovy, grated onion, French dressing. Serve in "boats."   *Banana-Pecan Pudding.* Recipe 143.

To delight the eye—a golden yellow and white casserole with sharp contrasts of olive black.

79   ORANGE-COCONUT CHICKEN CASSEROLE

Preheat oven to 350° F.
Oven time: 45-55 minutes   *6-8 servings*

2 cut-up broiling chickens, each about 3 pounds
    ready to cook
2 cloves garlic
6 tablespoons all-purpose flour
1½ teaspoons salt
¼ teaspoon pepper
½ teaspoon ginger
3 tablespoons shortening
4 navel oranges
1 tablespoon brown sugar
¾ cup shredded coconut
1 cup orange juice
2 tablespoons lemon juice
½ cup sliced black olives

Rub chicken pieces with garlic, then shake them, a few at a time, in paper bag with flour, salt, pepper, and ginger. Heat shortening in flameproof 2-quart casserole. Brown chicken on all sides. (Or use skillet then transfer to casserole.) Peel oranges, removing all membrane. Cut fruit into slices ½-inch thick, sprinkle with brown sugar, then tuck all around chicken. Toss in coconut. Combine orange and lemon juices, and sprinkle over bird. Cover tightly, put into oven, and bake until fork tender. Before serving, scatter olives into casserole.

NOTE: You may prefer to brown chicken right in oven. In that case, heat oven to 500° F., reduce to 375° as soon as chicken browns, and continue as directed.

If you like the Chinese style of cooking vegetables so they retain their crispness, this recipe will please you.

80   CHINESE PEPPER CHICKEN

Preheat oven to 375° F.
Oven time: about 45 minutes   *6-8 servings*

2 quartered broiling chickens, each about 3 pounds
    ready to cook
1 cup water
1 clove of garlic, mashed
3 tablespoons soy sauce
1 tablespoon sugar
1 teaspoon salt
2 tablespoons sherry wine
3 tablespoons oil
2 sweet peppers, seeded and cut into 1-inch squares
4 green onions (scallions) cut into 1-inch pieces
2 teaspoons celery salt

Wash and dry chicken. Combine water, garlic, soy sauce, sugar, salt and sherry in a flameproof 2-quart cast-iron casserole, and bring to a quick boil on surface range. (Or use saucepan and pour into casserole.) Add chicken, cover and cook for 20 minutes, then place in preheated oven and bake for 30 minutes. Remove cover and add peppers, green onions and celery seed. Continue baking, uncovered for about 15 minutes longer. Serve while greens are still crisp. Cooked rice is a fitting accompaniment.

CHINESE-STYLE BUFFET

How to manage: Bake cookies first. Remove from oven. Increase temperature to 450°. Bake spareribs for 30 minutes, reduce heat to 375°, add chicken, serve together.

Egg Rolls. Buy these frozen. Brown in oven about 25 minutes. Serve with English mustard.   *Barbecued Spareribs.* Recipe 72.   *Chinese Pepper Chicken.* Recipe 80. *Cooked Rice.*   *Almond Butter Cookies.* Recipe 133. *Spiced Kumquats.*   *Oolong Tea.*

OVEN MEAL: *Put into oven at same time, Favorite Chicken and Rice Loaf, Carrot Ring with Buttered Peas, Pineapple Brown Betty*, Recipe 149.

81   FAVORITE CHICKEN AND RICE LOAF

Preheat oven to 375° F.
Oven time: 45-55 minutes   *6-8 servings*

1 fowl, about 4 pounds ready to cook
4 medium carrots, scraped
3 stalks celery, washed
1½ cups cooked rice
2 eggs, slightly beaten
Salt
Pepper

Cook fowl in boiling salted water that just covers it. When barely tender, remove, skim broth and save for sauce. Let bird cool, then remove bones and put meat, carrots and celery through grinder, using fine blade. Add rice and eggs to ground mixture. Season with salt and pepper to taste. If it seems dry, add chicken broth. Shape mixture into loaf, and turn it into greased loaf pan or shallow baking dish about 2 or 2¼-quarts capacity. Bake until loaf is brown. Serve hot with Spinach Sauce.

SPINACH SAUCE: Make medium white sauce: melt 2 tablespoons butter; blend in 2 tablespoons flour. Slowly add ½ cup milk, ½ cup chicken broth, ½ teaspoon salt and a dash of pepper. Cook until sauce thickens, stirring to keep it smooth. Remove from heat. Blend in ½ cup cooked, finely chopped spinach, 2 teaspoons lemon juice, and a dash of nutmeg. Serve hot.

FOR INDIVIDUAL LOAVES

Divide chicken mixture into 6 or 8 casseroles. Shape mixture to fit. Bake until crisp.

Old-fashioned in flavor only—what could be more modern than a biscuit mix for potpie?

82   OLD-FASHIONED CHICKEN AND HAM POTPIE

Preheat oven to 450° F.
Oven time: 20 minutes   *4 servings*

1 cup prepared biscuit mix
⅓ cup milk
1 tablespoon onion juice
2 cups cooked chicken (meat of 3-pound bird)
⅓ cup cooked diced ham
½ cup cooked peas and carrots, drained
¼ teaspoon poultry dressing
2 cups gravy or medium white sauce made partly with
    chicken stock, partly with milk
Salt and pepper to taste

Mix biscuit mix, milk and onion juice (the latter is a *must* for a truly delicious flavor). Roll out dough to fit top of baking dish. (Turn dish upside down and measure dough.) Heat all other ingredients in saucepan. Pour into greased 1½-quart baking dish or casserole. Top with biscuit dough. Cut 2 or 3 slits in center for steam to escape. Bake in preheated oven until crust is golden brown.

83   CHICKEN PIE WITH PERFECT CRISPY CRUST

Bake biscuit dough without any filling. (Match dough to serving dish before baking.) Put hot seasoned chicken and sauce into serving dish, cover with baked crust, and bring to table. Perfect!

TO THAW FROZEN CHICKEN PIES

Place unthawed pies in oven heated to 400°, bake 20-30 minutes.

84   FABULOUS CHICKEN CURRY

Preheat oven to 350° F.
Oven time: about 40-50 minutes   *4-6 servings*

3 tablespoons butter or margarine
1 tart apple, pared, cored and finely chopped
1 small onion, finely chopped
1 tablespoon chutney
3 teaspoons curry powder (taste as you go, curry
    powders vary in strength)
2 cups chicken stock, leftover gravy, or bouillon cubes
    dissolved in hot water
1 cup milk
2 cups cooked chicken
1 cup raw rice

Melt butter or margarine, add apples and onions, and cook on surface range until onions are soft. Stir in chutney and curry powder, and cook for about 10 minutes until slightly thickened. Now pour in chicken stock and milk, and let heat. Put layers of chicken, rice and sauce into 2-quart casserole, cover and bake in oven until rice is done. Serve with as many extras as you can manage. I like to fill a huge tray with mounds of chopped coconut, cooked crumpled bacon, chopped hazelnuts, raisins and bananas (sliced raw or baked in the oven with the curry), chutney, avocado cubes, chopped hard-cooked eggs and onions, and banana muffins.

UNORTHODOX NOTE

Spread toast triangles with butter and coconut sirup. Spread melba toast rounds with garlic butter. Let get piping hot in oven. Alternate triangles and rounds to make border around curry.

85   DUCKLING BAKED IN CRANBERRY SAUCE

Preheat oven to 350° F.
Oven time: about 2 hours   *4-6 servings*

1 4-6 pound duckling, cut into 8 or 10 pieces
¼ cup butter or oil
1½ teaspoons salt
½ teaspoon paprika
2 cups cranberry sauce, fresh or canned
1 tablespoon lemon juice

Select a duckling which is not too fat, or cut away fat. Rub each piece with garlic. In large flameproof casserole which has a tight cover, heat the butter or oil, and brown bird on all sides. Sprinkle with salt and paprika. Cover casserole and bake for about 1½ hours. Remove all fat drippings from the pan. Combine cranberry sauce and lemon juice and pour over pieces. Cover and bake for ½ hour longer. Small tart apples, pared and cored, may be placed among the pieces during the last hour of baking.

WINTER DINNER FOR 4

How to manage: Start duckling and rice pudding in oven preheated to 350°. After 1 hour, add potatoes. Twenty minutes before they are ready, heat grapefruit (invert covers of casseroles to make place for them) and serve as soon as grapefruit is slightly browned.

Brandied Grapefruit. Sweet grapefruit halves (loosen sections first) with sugar, add a tablespoon of brandy to each half, heat for 15 minutes.   *Duckling Baked in Cranberry Sauce.* Recipe 85.   *Potatoes Royale With Swiss Cheese.* Recipe 106.   *Endive Salad With Chopped Hard Egg.   Garlic-Flavored French Dressing.   Country Rice Pudding.* Recipe 151.

7. Vegetables for all-in-one plate combinations

Time will vary depending on oven temperature, and whether asparagus was completely cooked.

86 ASPARAGUS AU GRATIN

Preheat oven to 375°-450° F.
Oven time: 15-30 minutes   *6 servings*

2 pounds asparagus, partly or completely cooked
1 can (10 ounces) condensed cream of asparagus soup
¼ cup milk or asparagus liquid
3 tablespoons buttered crumbs
3 tablespoons grated cheese

Arrange partly-cooked asparagus in buttered shallow baking dish. Cover with 1 can condensed cream of asparagus soup mixed with ¼ cup milk or liquid in which asparagus was cooked. Sprinkle with buttered crumbs and grated cheese, and bake uncovered until brown. Serve with sliced hard-cooked eggs.

87 GREEN BEANS IN CREAM

Preheat oven to 350°-400° F.
Oven time: 25-30 minutes   *4 servings*

Arrange 2 cups drained cooked green beans in buttered roaster vegetable pan. Combine ½ cup heavy cream, 1 tablespoon onion juice, 3 tablespoons butter, salt and pepper. Pour over beans. Dot with butter. Bake until piping hot.

88 SAVORY BEETS

Preheat oven to 375°-400° F.
Oven time: 1-1¼ hours   *6 servings*

Put 4 cups pared, thinly-sliced beets and 2 cups thinly-sliced onions into buttered 1½-quart casserole. Combine ½ cup orange juice, 3 tablespoons butter, 3 tablespoons sugar and 1 teaspoon salt. Pour into casserole, cover and bake until beets are tender.

89   BAKED BROCCOLI CHICAGO

Preheat oven to 400° F.
Oven time: 15-20 minutes   *4-6 servings*

2 cups milk
½ teaspoon caraway seeds
1 teaspoon marjoram
½ teaspoon thyme
½ teaspoon salt
2 pounds broccoli, washed
½ cup cubed cheese
¼ cup buttered coarse bread crumbs

Heat milk in saucepan. Add caraway seeds, marjoram, thyme, salt and broccoli. Cook for 10 minutes until just tender. Lift out vegetable with slotted spoon; transfer to baking dish. Add cheese to milk in saucepan, and let it melt. Pour over broccoli in baking dish, top with crumbs, and bake until bubbly.

90   CABBAGE POLONAISE

Preheat oven to 375°-425° F.
Oven time: 30-40 minutes   *6 servings*

Cut 2 pounds cabbage into thick wedges. Cook in boiling salted water until just tender. Arrange in buttered roaster vegetable pan. Combine ½ cup sour cream, 1 cup tomato sauce, 1 teaspoon onion, 1 tablespoon sugar, 1 teaspoon salt, and ¼ teaspoon pepper. Pour over cabbage. Bake uncovered, until done. Excellent served over rice.

91   SCALLOPED CAULIFLOWER IN PIMENTO SAUCE

Preheat oven to 375° F.
Oven time: about 15 minutes

Put into buttered baking dish, 2 cups cooked cauliflower, 1 cup medium cream sauce, 3 tablespoons finely-shredded pimentos. Top with fine bread crumbs. Bake uncovered, until bubbly. (Make cream sauce using part milk, part liquid from cauliflower.)

92   CARROT RINGS

Preheat oven to 350°-400° F.
Oven time: 30-40 minutes   *6 servings*

Mash 2 cups cooked carrots, blend in 1 can (10-ounce) condensed cream of celery soup, 2 tablespoons milk or vegetable
liquid, and turn into a buttered 1-quart ring mold. Set in pan of
hot water in oven, and bake until ring is firm. Loosen edges with
a knife, and invert ring on large platter. Fill center with cooked
buttered peas and mushrooms.

93   CORN SOUFFLÉ

Preheat oven to 350° F.
Oven time: 30-40 minutes   *6 servings*

2 tablespoons butter or margarine
2 tablespoons flour
½ cup chicken stock, or bouillon cube
½ cup milk
Salt and pepper
2 eggs, separated

Melt butter or margarine in skillet, stir in flour, then pour in
chicken stock, milk, salt and pepper. Cook gently for 10 minutes. Remove from flame. Stir some of the sauce into slightly-
beaten egg yolks, then spoon eggs back into remainder of sauce.
Combine with corn, fold in stiffly-beaten egg whites, turn into
buttered 1-quart casserole. Set casserole in pan of hot water in
oven, and bake until soufflé is firm.

94   BAKED CORN ON COB

Preheat oven to 400° F.
Oven time: 12-15 minutes

Remove outer husks and silk, leaving tender inner husks. Wash
quickly, dry, spread with butter. Replace inner husks, and bake.

95   EGGPLANT SOUFFLÉ

Preheat oven to 325° F.
Oven time: 40-50 minutes   *6 servings*

2 small eggplants
2 tablespoons butter
2 tablespoons flour
½ cup milk
½ cup light cream
3 tablespoons grated cheese
1 tablespoon catsup
1 teaspoon grated onion
2 egg yolks, beaten slightly
Salt and pepper
2 egg whites, beaten stiff

Pare eggplants, cut into slices 1-inch thick, and cook in boiling water until tender. Chop fine. Combine with butter, flour, milk, cream, grated cheese, catsup, onion, egg yolks, salt and pepper to taste. Fold in beaten egg whites. Turn into unbuttered 1½-quart casserole, and bake until firm.

96   EGGPLANT PARMIGIANA

Preheat oven to 375°-400° F.
Oven time: 20-30 minutes   *4-6 servings*

Cut an eggplant into slices ¼-inch thick. Combine 1 slightly beaten egg, 1 tablespoon water, salt, pepper, and a dash of grated cheese. Dip eggplant in mixture. Heat oil in skillet. Brown mashed clove of garlic and eggplant. Transfer eggplant to platter, discard garlic. Heat 2 cups tomatoes to boiling in same skillet. In shallow baking dish, spread a layer of sauce, a layer of browned eggplant, and slices of Mozzarella cheese. Repeat layers, ending with tomato sauce. Top with grated Parmesan cheese, and bake uncovered, until bubbling hot.

97   BAKED MUSHROOMS IN CREAM

Preheat oven to 400°-450° F.
Oven time: 10-15 minutes   *6 servings*

2 pounds mushrooms
½ cup heavy cream
4 tablespoons butter
2 teaspoons onion
1 tablespoon chopped parsley
Salt and pepper

Brush mushrooms, peel them if they are tough. Remove stems, and place mushroom caps, rounded side up, in buttered shallow baking dish. Make as many layers as necessary. Combine other ingredients, pour over mushrooms, cover and bake until done. Serve on buttered toast with any juices left in pan.

98   ONION AND APPLE CASSEROLE

Preheat oven to 350°-400° F.
Oven time: 45-60 minutes   *4 servings*

2 tablespoons butter or margarine
3 tablespoons flour
4 tablespoons brown sugar
½ teaspoon salt
¼ teaspoon nutmeg
4 tart green apples
3 small onions

Make sauce: In skillet, melt butter, stir in flour, add brown sugar, salt, nutmeg and 1 cup water. Cook for a few minutes. Peel, core, and slice apples. Peel and cut onions into thin slices. In a buttered 2-quart casserole, overlap onions and apples to make one layer. Spoon sauce over the layer. Repeat layers and sauce. Bake, covered, until apples and onions are tender. Remove cover for last 10 minutes.

99   GLAZED ONIONS

Preheat oven to 350° F.
Oven time: about 20 minutes   *4 servings*

1 pound small white onions
3 tablespoons butter
3 tablespoons flour
1 tablespoon sugar

Cook onions in boiling salted water to cover, until barely tender. Drain, save liquid. Turn onions into buttered shallow casserole or roaster vegetable pan. Melt butter in skillet, stir in flour, add 2 tablespoons liquid in which onions were cooked, and pour over onions. Bake uncovered until onions are glazed.

100   PIMENTOES RANCHERO

Preheat oven to 400° F.
Oven time: 12-15 minutes   *1 pimento per serving*

Fill a raw pimento with creamed potatoes, top with grated cheese, put in greased shallow baking pan or vegetable dish, and bake until tender. Dust with paprika before serving. (To cream potatoes, cook whole new potatoes in boiling salted water. When tender, slip off skins, cube potatoes, and combine them with one-half their measure of medium white sauce.)

101   STUFFED GREEN PEPPERS

Preheat oven to 400° F.
Oven time: 12-15 minutes   *6 servings*

Select 6 chunky peppers, discard stem end and seeds, and parboil peppers for a few minutes. Combine 1½ cups grated cheese and 1½ cups soft bread crumbs. Season with salt, pepper, butter or margarine, and a few teaspoons onion juice. Spoon into peppers, top with fine buttered crumbs, and bake until tops are brown.

To bake potatoes with a soft, moist skin, brush them with fat after washing. For a crisp skin, leave dry.

102   BAKED POTATOES

Preheat oven to 375°-425° F.
Oven time: 45-55 minutes

Select slender potatoes, scrub and dry them. Bake until tender. Make a crisscross cut in skin, and press until potato pulp pops out. Add a teaspoon of butter, salt and paprika. To reduce baking time, cut potatoes in half, brush with butter, and bake, cut side down, in shallow pan.

103   CLUB POTATOES

Scoop out pulp from baked potatoes. Mash with milk, cream, butter, and chopped, cooked ham. Spoon back into shell. Bake until tops are brown. About 15 minutes at 400° F.

104   PARSLEY POTATOES

Preheat oven to 375°-425° F.
Oven time: about 1 hour

Scrub small potatoes. Put into vegetable baking dish, add ¼-inch water, and bake uncovered until tender. While still hot, remove skins and roll potatoes in parsley butter (melted butter combined with lots of chopped parsley).

105   POTATOES WITH A ROAST

Allow about 1¾-2 hours of cooking for raw peeled potatoes placed alongside roast at low temperature. To reduce time, cook whole potatoes about 10 minutes in boiling salted water. Peel, then put around roast. Potatoes will be done within an hour.

106   POTATOES ROYALE WITH SWISS CHEESE

Preheat oven to 350° F.
Oven time: about 1 hour

In a shallow casserole, arrange a layer of sliced raw potatoes. Dot with butter, top with slices of Swiss cheese. Repeat layers. Bake in oven until potatoes are soft. Do not bake in oven above 350° F. or cheese will become stringy.

107   OVEN "FRENCH-FRIED" POTATOES

Preheat oven to 450° F.
Oven time: about 30 minutes

Cut potatoes into long thin strips. Soak in cold water for half an hour, drain and dry. Brush with oil, and spread out on baking sheet. Bake in preheated oven until potatoes are brown. Turn them once to brown other side. They'll taste like those fried in deep fat. Easy and quick!

108   POTATO SCALLOP

Preheat oven to 350°-425° F.
Oven time: 40-50 minutes   *6 servings*

4 medium potatoes
2 medium onions, sliced
3 tablespoons grated cheese
Salt and pepper
2 tablespoons butter
1 cup light cream
Buttered bread crumbs

Cut potatoes into slices ¼-inch thick, and arrange in a buttered casserole. Sprinkle with onions, then grated cheese. Season each layer with salt and pepper. Dot with butter. Repeat layers. Pour in cream, top with buttered crumbs, and bake uncovered, until tender.

109   BAKED SWEET POTATOES

Preheat oven to 375°-425° F.
Oven time: 45-55 minutes

Scrub sweet potatoes, dry them, place on oven rack, and bake until tender. To remove steam, cut cross in each potato, and press out pulp.

110   SWEET POTATO PIE

Preheat oven to 425° F.
Oven time: about 25 minutes   *4 servings*

2 cups cooked sweet potatoes
1 egg, slightly beaten
3 tablespoons butter or margarine
3 tablespoons milk
¼ teaspoon salt
¼ cup sugar
1 teaspoon grated lemon rind
¼ teaspoon nutmeg
Pastry dough (Recipe 135)

Mash sweet potatoes with egg, butter, milk, and salt. Line an 8- or 9-inch pie plate with pastry dough, top with potato mixture, and bake uncovered, until top is brown and oozing with juice. (This can be made also as a pudding without pie dough.)

111   CANDIED SWEETS

Preheat oven to 375°-425° F.
Oven time: 25-35 minutes   *6 servings*

6 sweet potatoes, cooked in their skins
¼ cup brown sugar
3 tablespoons butter or margarine
3 tablespoons honey

Peel potatoes. Cut in half lengthwise, and arrange in greased, shallow baking pan. Combine other ingredients, and spoon over potatoes. Bake until brown and glazed.

112   LOUISIANA SWEET POTATO CASSEROLE

Preheat oven to 375°-425° F.
Oven time: 25-35 minutes

Arrange in layers: sliced cooked sweet potatoes, cooked whole-kernel corn, sliced peeled bananas, molasses, brown sugar, and butter. Bake uncovered in buttered casserole until brown.

113   SWEET POTATO AND PINEAPPLE

Preheat oven to 375°-425° F.
Oven time: 25-35 minutes

Peel 6 cooked sweet potatoes, cut into slices, and arrange in greased shallow casserole. Spoon 1 cup canned crushed pineapple over them. Add 3 tablespoons brown sugar, and dot with 3 tablespoons butter. Bake until bubbly.

114   SQUASH AND APPLE CASSEROLE

Preheat oven to 375°-400° F.
Oven time: 40-50 minutes   *4-6 servings*

2 pounds squash
1 pound tart apples, pared and cored
¼ cup butter or margarine
2 tablespoons onion juice
½ teaspoon salt
3 tablespoons slivered almonds

Cut squash into slices ½-inch thick. Cut apples into rings 1-inch thick. Arrange a layer of squash, and a layer of apples in a greased 2½-quart casserole. Combine butter, onion juice, and salt, and sprinkle over each layer. Top with almonds, and bake until squash and apples are tender.

115   BAKED WINTER SQUASH

Preheat oven to 350°-400° F.
Oven time: 50-60 minutes   *1 pound serves 3*

Scrub whole squash and put into oven in its own shell to bake until tender. When soft, cut in half, scoop out seeds, add butter, and season with salt and pepper. Fill centers with hot, cooked peas or other seasoned cooked vegetable, or serve plain.

116   BAKED DEVILED TOMATOES

Preheat oven to 400°-450° F.
Oven time: 8-10 minutes   *4 servings*

Select 4 firm tomatoes of equal size. Cut in half. Combine 1 tablespoon grated onion, 1 teaspoon dry mustard, salt and paprika, and spread over each half, pushing seasoning into tomatoes. Dot with butter. Bake uncovered in shallow baking pan.

117   CREOLE TOMATOES

Preheat oven to 375°-425° F.
Oven time: 15-25 minutes   *6 servings*

6 tomatoes
1 small can sliced mushrooms
1 tablespoon chopped onion
1 tablespoon chopped green pepper
1 cup soft bread crumbs
1 teaspoon salt
½ teaspoon pepper
1 tablespoon lemon juice
3 tablespoons butter

Scoop out pulp from tomatoes, leaving thick shell. Invert and drain. Chop pulp. Melt butter in skillet, add mushrooms and onions. When brown, add pulp, crumbs, salt, pepper, and lemon juice. Fill tomatoes with mixture, dot with butter, and bake in shallow pan until tomatoes are tender.

8. Hot breads, cakes and pies

A moist bread that toasts unusually well. Try it!

118   BANANA TEA BREAD

Preheat oven to 350° F.
Oven time: 1 hour 15 minutes   *1 loaf*

1¾ cups sifted flour
2 teaspoons baking powder
¼ teaspoon baking soda
½ teaspoon salt
⅓ cup shortening
⅔ cup sugar
2 eggs, well beaten
1 cup mashed ripe bananas (2-3 bananas)

Sift together flour, baking powder, baking soda and salt. In mixing bowl, beat shortening until creamy. Gradually add sugar and continue beating until light and fluffy. Add eggs and beat well. Add flour mixture alternately with bananas, a little at a time, beating after each addition until smooth. Turn into a well-greased bread pan 8½ x 4½ x 3 inches, and bake until bread is done.

119   DATE-NUT BREAD

Preheat oven to 350° F.
Oven time about 1 hour   *1 loaf*

Sift together 3 cups sifted all-purpose flour, 4 teaspoons baking powder, 1 cup sugar, 1½ teaspoons salt. Cut in ¼ cup shortening. Combine 1 egg, and 1 cup milk, then add to first mixture. Add 1 cup broken nut meats, and 1 cup finely-cut dates, and mix thoroughly. Pour into greased 9" x 5" x 3" loaf pan. Bake until done.

120   PRUNE AND APRICOT NUT LOAF

Substitute ¾ cup finely-chopped prunes, and ¼ cup dried apricots for the dates. Proceed as above.

121   OLD-FASHIONED SOUR CREAM CORN BREAD

Preheat oven to 425° F.
Oven time: about 30 minutes   *1 loaf*

¾ cup sifted all-purpose flour
1 teaspoon baking powder
½ teaspoon baking soda
1 teaspoon salt
1 tablespoon sugar
1 cup yellow corn meal
1 egg, slightly beaten
½ cup milk
1 cup commercial sour cream
1 tablespoon melted butter or shortening

Sift together flour, baking powder, baking soda, salt and sugar.
Add cornmeal. Combine egg, milk, sour cream and butter; add
to dry ingredients. Blend well. Bake in buttered 8″ x 8″ x 2″ pan.

122   BUTTERMILK CORN MEAL ROLLS

Preheat oven to 450° F.
Oven time: about 12 minutes   *10-12 rolls*

1½ cups sifted all-purpose flour
¾ cup yellow corn meal
1 tablespoon baking powder
1 tablespoon sugar
1 teaspoon salt
¼ teaspoon baking soda
2 tablespoons shortening
1 egg, well beaten
½ cup buttermilk
Melted butter

Sift together first 6 ingredients. Cut in shortening. Mix egg and
milk; add to sifted ingredients. Roll out ½ inch thick. Cut into
rounds with 3-inch biscuit cutter. Brush with melted butter, fold
over, bake on greased cooky sheet.

123   EASY OATMEAL BREAD

Preheat oven to 350° F.
Oven time: about 1 hour   *2 loaves*

1¾ cups boiling water
1 cup rolled oats
½ cup light molasses
½ cup milk
1 teaspoon salt
1 cake compressed yeast (or 1 package dry yeast dissolved
    in boiling water. Subtract water used from amount to
    be poured over oatmeal)
5 cups sifted all-purpose flour

Pour water over rolled oats and let cool until lukewarm. Mix in
molasses, milk, salt and yeast. Gradually blend in flour. Place
dough in greased bowl, cover and store in refrigerator for 3
hours. Shape the cold dough into 2 loaves and place in greased
pans 9" x 4" x 3". Cover pans and let dough rise for about 2 hours
in a warm place. Bulk will double. Bake until brown.

124   EMPANADAS

Preheat oven to 400° F.
Oven time: 15-20 minutes   *12-15 empanadas*

2 cups sifted all-purpose flour
2 tablespoons sugar
2 teaspoons baking powder
½ teaspoon salt
6 tablespoons lard or butter
1 egg yolk
¼ cup ice-cold water
1½ cups corned beef-hash, creamed chicken or lobster

Sift together flour, sugar, baking powder and salt. Cut in shortening. Add egg yolk, then ice water, a little at a time. Roll out
thin. Cut into 3-inch rounds with a biscuit cutter or a glass. Top
with 1 heaping tablespoon of cooked meat or fish. Fold dough
in half, moisten edges and press tightly together. Bake.

125   RICH CREAM BISCUITS

Preheat oven to 450° F.
Oven time: 12-15 minutes   *14 biscuits*

Sift together 2 cups sifted all-purpose flour, 2 teaspoons baking powder, ½ teaspoon salt. Add 1 cup heavy cream to make a soft dough. Roll out ½-inch thick, cut into rounds with a 2-inch cutter. Put on ungreased baking sheet, close together for soft biscuits, far apart for crusty ones. To make very crusty biscuits, roll dough ¼-inch thick.

BISCUIT VARIATIONS

Plain Biscuits. Sift 2 cups all purpose flour, 3 teaspoons baking powder. Cut in ½ cup shortening. Quickly add ¾ cup milk. Turn out on floured board. Knead. Roll out ½-inch thick (¼-inch if you like thin biscuits . . . you'll have twice as many). Cut with biscuit cutter. Bake on ungreased cooky sheet as above.

Buttermilk Biscuits. Use 2 teaspoons baking powder and ¼ teaspoon soda instead of 3 teaspoons baking powder. Use sour milk or buttermilk instead of milk.

Cheese Biscuits. Add ½ cup grated sharp cheese, 2 tablespoons minced green pepper, and 2 tablespoons chopped pimentos after cutting shortening into flour.

Bacon Biscuits. Add ½ cup crisp crumpled bacon to shortening.

Parsley Biscuits. Cut in ¼ cup chopped parsley with shortening.

Orange Marmalade Biscuits. Add 2 teaspoons orange marmalade to mixture after cutting in shortening.

Pinwheel Biscuits. Roll biscuit mixture ¼ inch thick. Brush it with melted butter. Roll up as jelly roll. Cut off slices ¾ inch thick. Bake as above.

Filled Biscuits. Roll biscuit mixture ¼ inch thick. Cut with biscuit cutter. Top half the biscuits with very finely chopped ham, cooked onions, grated cheese, minced cooked chicken, etc. Cover with remaining biscuits. Press together lightly.

126   POPOVERS THAT POP

Preheat oven to 425° F.
Oven time: about 40 minutes   *10-12 popovers*

1 cup sifted all-purpose flour
¼ teaspoon salt
1 tablespoon melted butter
1 cup milk
2 eggs

Sift together flour and salt. Add butter, milk and eggs and beat about 3 minutes until batter is very smooth. Pour into well-greased muffin or popover pans (allow about ½ teaspoon butter for each cup) until cups are half full. Bake 30 minutes, turn off oven, prick popovers with a fork to let steam escape, then leave them in the oven for about 10 minutes to dry out.

POPOVER POINTERS

Be sure batter is smooth.
Be sure to prick them so steam escapes. If they are not allowed to dry out, they will sag when cool.
Fill popovers with creamed chicken, lobster, or other fillings to serve as main course at luncheon. They are handsome and festive.

127   PARKER HOUSE ROLLS

Preheat oven to 425° F.
Oven time: about 12-15 minutes   *12 rolls*

2½ cups sifted all-purpose flour
1 tablespoon sugar
1 teaspoon salt
2 tablespoons shortening
1 package dry or compressed yeast
⅓ cup lukewarm water
½ cup milk

Sift together flour, sugar and salt. Blend in shortening. Dissolve yeast in water, add to milk, and combine with sifted dry ingredients. Mix thoroughly. Let rise in warm place until double in bulk (about 1 hour). Roll out ⅓ inch thick. Cut into rounds with a 3-inch cutter; brush with melted butter; fold approximately in half with larger part underneath. Brush tops with melted butter and bake until golden brown.

128   BANANA LAYER CAKE

Preheat oven to 375° F.
Oven time: 30-40 minutes

2¼ cups sifted cake flour
1¼ cups sugar
2½ teaspoons baking powder
½ teaspoon baking soda
½ teaspoon salt
½ cup shortening (brought to room temperature)
1½ cups (4 or 5) mashed ripe bananas
2 eggs
1 teaspoon vanilla

In large bowl, sift together flour, sugar, baking powder, soda and salt. Add shortening, ½ cup bananas, and 2 eggs. Beat 2 minutes at slow to medium speed with electric mixer, or 3 minutes by hand. Scrape bowl and beater frequently while mixing.

Add remainder of bananas and vanilla. Beat 1 minute longer, scraping bowl and beater several times. Turn into 2 well-greased 8-inch layer cake pans. Bake until layers are done. Top with coconut, strawberry or pineapple frosting.

129   BANANA SPICE LAYERS

Sift ⅛ teaspoon ground cloves, 1¼ teaspoons cinnamon, ½ teaspoon nutmeg with flour and other dry ingredients. Proceed as above, or make in 18 well-greased cupcake pans.

130   QUICK CHOCOLATE CAKE

Preheat oven to 375° F.
Oven time: 25-30 minutes   2 cakes

1¾ cups sifted cake flour
2 teaspoons baking powder
¼ cup cocoa
½ teaspoon salt
½ cup butter or shortening
1½ cups granulated sugar
2 egg yolks, well beaten
1 cup milk
1 teaspoon vanilla
2 egg whites, beaten until stiff

Sift together flour, baking powder, cocoa, and salt. With back of spoon work shortening in bowl until smooth. Work in sugar. Stir in beaten egg yolks. Add dry ingredients alternately with milk, beating with each addition. Stir in vanilla, fold in egg whites. Bake in greased 8-inch cake pans.

MOCHA ICING: Blend together 2 cups confectioner's sugar, 3 tablespoons cocoa, 1 tablespoon butter, and 1 teaspoon vanilla. Gradually add enough strong black coffee to make of spreading consistency. (You will need about 2 tablespoons.) Spread on cakes.

Upside-down cakes are favorites. For variety use this basic recipe, substituting canned whole apricots and apricot sirup, or cooked peach halves and peach sirup for the pineapple.

131   UPSIDE-DOWN PINEAPPLE CAKE

Preheat oven to 350° F.
Oven time: 40-50 minutes

¼ cup butter or margarine
¾ cup light brown sugar
8 slices canned pineapple, well drained
⅓ cup shortening
⅔ cup sugar
1 egg
1⅓ cups sifted all-purpose flour
½ teaspoon soda
1 teaspoon baking powder
¼ teaspoon salt
½ cup pineapple sirup
1 tablespoon lemon juice

Melt butter or margarine in oven in 10″ x 12″ x 2½″ baking pan. Remove pan, spread butter evenly, sprinkle with brown sugar. Arrange pineapple over sugar. To make cake, cream shortening and sugar until light and fluffy. Beat in egg. Sift together flour, soda, baking powder, and salt. Add alternately with pineapple sirup and lemon juice to the creamed mixture. Spread cake batter over the fruit mixture in the pan, and bake until done. Cool for 5 minutes, loosen edges of cake, and invert by placing large plate over the pan and turning quickly so that pineapple and sugar mixture stay on top of the cake. Place maraschino cherry in center of each pineapple slice. Serve hot or cold.

132   WALNUT AND APRICOT LOAF

Preheat oven to 350° F.
Oven time: 45-50 minutes

⅔ cup shortening
1 cup sugar
2 eggs, separated
1¾ cups sifted all-purpose flour
½ teaspoon salt
2 teaspoons baking powder
½ cup milk
1 teaspoon vanilla extract
½ cup moist dried apricots
½ cup walnuts, coarsely chopped

Cream shortening and sugar until well blended, then beat in egg yolks one at a time. Sift together flour, salt and baking powder. Add alternately with milk and sugar to first mixture. Cut up apricots and mix with nut meats. Add to batter, then fold in stiffly beaten (but not dry) egg whites. Turn into well-greased loaf pan, and bake. When done, let stand a few minutes, loosen sides, and invert on a rack to cool.

133   ALMOND BUTTER COOKIES

Preheat oven to 350° F.
Oven time: 20 minutes   *about 6 dozen*

1 cup butter or margarine
3 tablespoons confectioner's sugar
1 teaspoon vanilla extract
⅛ teaspoon almond extract
2 cups sifted all-purpose flour
1 cup diced roasted almonds
Confectioner's sugar for rolling

Cream butter and confectioner's sugar together until well blended, then add vanilla and almond extracts. Stir in flour and almonds. Mix. Shape into small balls, put on ungreased cooky sheet and bake. While still hot, roll in confectioner's sugar.

134   PEANUT COOKIES

Preheat oven to 375° F.
Oven time: 13-16 minutes   *about 6 dozen*

2 cups sifted all-purpose flour
3 teaspoons baking powder
½ teaspoon salt
½ cup butter or margarine
1 cup sugar
2 eggs, slightly beaten
1 cup chopped peanuts

Sift together flour, baking powder and salt. Cream butter and
sugar, add eggs and peanuts and combine with sifted ingredients.
Shape dough into balls the size of walnuts. Press with a fork to
make crisscross pattern, and bake on cooky sheet until brown.

When baking 2 pies at one time in your roaster oven, allow
maximum baking times. Temperature settings may be in-
creased 25° if pies are not browning properly.

135   FLAKY PIE SHELLS

See oven temperature below
Makes 2 8-inch pastry shells

1½ cups sifted all-purpose flour
½ teaspoon salt
½ cup shortening
4 tablespoons cold water

Sift together flour and salt. Cut in shortening to make coarse
mixture. Add water a little at a time, pushing moistened dough
to one side. When all particles are moistened, gather dough into
ball. Chill for half an hour (it can be wrapped in waxed paper
and refrigerated for several days). Roll out on floured board.
Follow directions below:

FOR PIE SHELLS TO BE FILLED BEFORE BAKING: Follow recipe for oven temperature. Line 2 ungreased 8-inch pie plates with dough. Do not prick dough. Fill shell and bake according to recipe directions.

FOR PIE SHELLS TO BE BAKED BEFORE FILLING: Preheat oven to 450° F. Line 2 ungreased 8-inch pie plates with dough. With a fork prick shells all over to force out air. Refrigerate for 15 minutes; prick dough again. Bake in preheated oven until shells are golden. When done, cool on rack without removing from plates. Fill according to recipe directions.

136   SPICY APPLE PIE

Preheat oven to 425° F.
Oven time: 35-40 minutes   *1 8-inch pie*

2 Flaky Pie Shells, Recipe 135
5-6 cups tart apples, pared and diced
⅔ cup brown sugar
2 teaspoons lemon juice
1 teaspoon cinnamon
½ teaspoon nutmeg
2 tablespoons butter or margarine

Divide Flaky Pie Shells into 2 uneven portions. Roll out the slightly larger portion to line an 8-inch pie plate. Refrigerate remainder of dough. Place half of apples in plate. Combine sugar, lemon juice, cinnamon and nutmeg. Toss half of mixture over apples. Top with remaining apples and seasonings. Dot with butter or margarine. Roll out remaining dough to fit pie plate, allowing 1-inch extra edge. Make slits in center with fork. Moisten rim of bottom crust with cold water. Press top and bottom rims together. Bake until apples are tender when tested with a toothpick.

137   LOUISIANA PECAN PIE

Preheat oven to 400° F.
Oven time: 40-50 minutes

½ recipe Flaky Pie Shells, Recipe 135

Beat 3 eggs slightly. Add 1 cup sugar, 1 cup dark corn sirup, 1 cup shelled unsalted whole pecans, 1 teaspoon vanilla, and 1 teaspoon salt. Pour into 8-inch unbaked pie shell. Bake in preheated oven for 10 minutes, then reduce oven to 300° F. to finish.

> *Sugared and spiced berries are so good under a flaky pastry top. Canned fruit can be used too, but then reduce sugar to ¾ cup.*

138   DEEP-DISH BLUEBERRY PIE

Preheat oven to 425° F.
Oven time: 40 minutes   *6-8 servings*

4 cups blueberries
1 cup sugar
3 tablespoons all-purpose flour
1 tablespoon lemon juice
1 tablespoon melted butter
1½ cups sifted all-purpose flour
½ teaspoon salt
½ cup shortening
4-5 tablespoons cold water

Combine berries, sugar, flour, lemon juice and butter. Stir gently to avoid crushing the berries. Pour into a square 10″ or 12″ pie pan. Let this stand for several minutes while you make pastry. Sift flour and salt, and cut in shortening. Add water slowly until dough is of good consistency. Gather into a ball, roll out on lightly floured board. Fit dough to top of baking dish, allowing ½ inch extra edge all around. Fold edge onto rim of dish, pressing it with a floured fork. Gash top so steam can escape. If you like glazed pie, brush pastry with top milk. Bake until brown. Cut into squares. Serve with whipped cream into which several berries have been crushed.

9. Desserts fresh from the oven

139   APPLE-NOODLE CHARLOTTE

Preheat oven to 350°-400° F.
Oven time: 30-40 minutes   *4 servings*

8 ounces broad noodles
1 egg, slightly beaten
1 cup seedless raisins
¾ cup sugar
¼ teaspoon cinnamon
2 large apples, pared, cored and thinly sliced
4 tablespoons butter

Cook noodles in boiling salted water until just tender. Drain.
Gently stir in egg. Combine raisins, sugar and cinnamon. In a
well-buttered 1½-quart casserole arrange a layer of noodles and
egg, a layer of raisin-cinnamon mixture, and a layer of apples.
Dot with butter. Repeat layers. Bake uncovered until top is
brown and crisp.

140   BAKED APPLES IN MAPLE SYRUP

Preheat oven to 375° F.-400° F.
Oven time: 45-55 minutes   *4 servings*

Wash and core 4 medium apples. Pare about ½ inch from top.
Fill centers with butter, maple sirup and cinnamon. Add 1 cup
water to baking pan. Bake uncovered until tender. Serve with
cream or, when apples are almost done, put a marshmallow on
each one, and serve as soon as marshmallow melts and browns.

141   OREGON APPLE PUDDING

Preheat oven to 375°-400° F.
Oven time: 50-60 minutes   *6 servings*

6 medium apples, pared, cored and chopped
3 egg yolks, slightly beaten
½ cup chopped almonds
½ cup cracker crumbs
½ cup sugar
2 tablespoons butter
1 teaspoon powdered cinnamon
4 ounces Bacardi rum
3 egg whites, beaten until stiff

Combine apples, egg yolks, almonds, crumbs, sugar, butter, cinnamon and rum. Stir until very well blended. Fold in egg whites.
Turn into buttered square pan and bake until brown. Serve hot
or cold.

142   APRICOT FLUFF

Preheat oven to 325° F.
Oven time: 30-40 minutes   *4 servings*

1 cup cooked apricots
¼ cup sugar
3 tablespoons orange juice
2 tablespoons lemon juice
1 teaspoon grated lemon rind
½ cup broken nut meats
2 egg whites

Put cooked apricots through a strainer, add sugar, orange and
lemon juices, lemon rind and nuts. Beat egg whites until stiff,
fold into apricot mixture, then turn into an 8- or 9-inch pie plate.
Bake uncovered until firm. Serve with custard sauce.

143   BANANA-PECAN PUDDING

Preheat oven to 375°-400° F.
Oven time: about 40 minutes   *6 servings*

1½ cups stale cake crumbs or soft bread crumbs
    (crusts removed)
2 cups milk
½ cup sugar
½ teaspoon vanilla
2 bananas, sliced
3 tablespoons melted butter
2 eggs, slightly beaten
¼ teaspoon salt
¾ cup chopped pecans

Soak crumbs in milk. Combine with other ingredients, tossing
lightly with a fork until well blended. Turn into a greased 1½-
quart casserole or baking dish. Put on rack and bake uncovered.
Serve hot with or without cream.

144   BAKED BANANAS

Preheat oven to 375° F.
Oven time: about 15-20 minutes   *6 servings*

Cut off tip ends of firm, partly-green bananas. Pull away one
long strip of peel from each, about one inch wide. Brush exposed
portions of bananas with butter. Sprinkle with salt. Place in
shallow dish and bake until bananas are tender and peels dis-
colored. Serve as vegetable or dessert.

145   SOUFFLÉED BANANA IN SHELL

Preheat oven to 375° F.
Oven time: 15 minutes   *6 servings*

Cut unpeeled bananas in half lengthwise. Remove pulp from the
skins and set skins aside for filling later. Mash pulp with a fork or
put it through a sieve. Beat one white of egg until stiff, then fold
into the mashed bananas. Fill empty skins with the mixture.
Place in shallow pan and set in oven to bake until slightly brown.

146   COCONUT CUP CUSTARD

Preheat oven to 325° F.
Oven time: 50-60 minutes   *4 servings*

3 eggs, beaten until light
4 tablespoons sugar
Dash of salt
1 cup shredded coconut
2 cups light cream
Nutmeg

Combine eggs, sugar and salt, stirring to dissolve the sugar. Stir in coconut, then milk. Pour into buttered custard cups. Sprinkle with nutmeg. Set in pan of hot water which comes ⅔ of the way to the tops of the cups. Bake until done. (A knife inserted in center of custard should come out clean.) Serve in custard cups.

147   LEMON CHIFFON PUDDING

Preheat oven to 350° F.
Oven time: 50-60 minutes   *6 servings*

6 tablespoons sifted all-purpose flour
1 cup sugar
¼ teaspoon salt
3 tablespoons butter
3 egg yolks, beaten until thick
3 tablespoons lemon juice
2 teaspoons grated lemon rind
1 cup milk
3 egg whites, beaten until stiff

Sift together flour, sugar, and salt. Cut in butter, add egg yolks, lemon juice, rind, and milk. Fold in egg whites. Pour into buttered 1½-quart baking dish, set in pan of hot water so that dish is immersed halfway. Bake until pudding is firm.

148   ORANGE-COCONUT PUDDING

Preheat oven to 350° F.
Oven time: about 1 hour   *6 servings*

3 tablespoons butter
1 cup sugar
4 egg yolks, slightly beaten
⅓ cup orange juice
1 tablespoon grated orange rind
¼ teaspoon salt
1¼ cups shredded coconut
2 tablespoons all-purpose flour
1 cup milk
4 egg whites, beaten until stiff

Cream together butter and sugar. Add yolks and beat well.
Blend in orange juice, rind and salt. Gently stir in 1 cup coconut
and flour, then milk. Fold in egg whites. Pour into 1½-quart
casserole set in a pan containing hot water. (Casserole should be
immersed at least halfway.) Bake until golden brown. Meanwhile
toast remaining coconut in a shallow pan; serve over pudding.

149   PINEAPPLE BROWN BETTY

Preheat oven to 375° F.
Oven time: 40-50 minutes   *6 servings*

3 cups pineapple chunks, drained
1⅓ cups soft bread crumbs
⅓ cup sugar
1 teaspoon cinnamon
2 tablespoons butter
2 tablespoons grated lemon peel
⅓ cup pineapple sirup

Place 1½ cups of the pineapple chunks in a casserole. Combine
bread crumbs, sugar and cinnamon. Sprinkle half of the mixture
over the pineapple. Dot with 1 tablespoon butter. Repeat with
the remaining pineapple, bread crumbs and butter. Sprinkle with
lemon peel, and pour pineapple sirup over all. Bake until done.

150   RHUBARB AND PINEAPPLE MERINGUE

Preheat oven to 350° F.
Oven time: 15-20 minutes   *6 servings*

2 cups soft bread crumbs (crusts removed)
2 tablespoons butter
1 cup cooked sweetened rhubarb
1 cup crushed pineapple
2 egg whites
2 tablespoons powdered sugar

Combine bread crumbs with butter in skillet and let brown. In a greased baking dish in alternate layers arrange crumbs, rhubarb and pineapple. Beat egg whites until they form a peak. Add powdered sugar and beat again until egg whites are stiff. Pile on fruit. Bake uncovered until top is golden brown.

151   COUNTRY RICE PUDDING

Preheat oven to 325° F.
Oven time: about 2-2½ hours   *4-6 servings*

6 tablespoons raw rice, washed
4 cups milk
¼ cup sugar
¼ teaspoon salt
¼ teaspoon nutmeg
Grated rind of ½ lemon
½ cup seedless raisins (optional)
2 eggs, slightly beaten

Combine all ingredients except raisins and eggs, and pour into greased 1½-quart casserole or baking dish. Bake until rice is done, stirring three or four times. After 1½ hours, add raisins and eggs, and continue baking until pudding is done.

152   OVEN COMPOTE OF FRUIT

Preheat oven to 350° F.
Oven time: about 1 hour   *12 servings*

1 pound dried apricots
½ pound peaches
½ pound pears
½ cup hot water
½ cup sugar
2 tablespoons rum

Combine all ingredients in casserole. Cover and bake in oven until fruits are tender.

153   PRUNES *AU* VIN

Preheat oven to 300° F.
Oven time: 1 hour   *6 servings*

In an ovenware bean pot or casserole, cover 1 pound large prunes with claret wine, ½ cup sugar, dash of nutmeg and lemon juice. Refrigerate for several hours. Cover and bake until prunes are tender. To thicken sirup, remove prunes and bake without cover, until reduced. Serve hot or cold.

154   PRUNE SOUFFLÉ

Preheat oven to 300° F.
Oven time: about 1 hour   *4-6 servings*

1 cup prune pulp (about 1 pound cooked pitted prunes
        put through a sieve)
1 tablespoon lemon juice
½ cup broken nut meats
½ cup fine dry bread crumbs
2 tablespoons sugar
¼ teaspoon salt
¼ teaspoon cinnamon
3 tablespoons prune juice
2 eggs, separated
Grated rind of 1 lemon

Pour lemon juice over prune pulp. Combine nuts, crumbs, sugar, salt, cinnamon and prune juice and add to prunes. Beat egg yolks well, add with rind to prunes. Fold in stiffly-beaten egg whites. Turn into a greased 9-inch baking dish. Set it in pan of hot water and bake until soufflé is firm. Serve hot with lemon or custard sauce.

LEMON SAUCE

½ cup sugar
1 tablespoon cornstarch
1 cup boiling water
2 tablespoons butter
1½ tablespoons lemon juice
Pinch of salt and nutmeg

In a saucepan, combine sugar and cornstarch, then stir in water. Boil 5 minutes. Add other ingredients. Serve hot. About 1½ cups.

10. *About your broiler griddle*

HOW TO USE YOUR INFRA-RED BROILER ATTACHMENT FOR BROILING

Assemble broiler-grill as directed by manufacturer. Adjust rack to recommended distance. For easier clean-up, use a shallow broiling pan (and rack, if recipe directs), set on large oven rack. Preheat broiler 4 minutes. Grease pan or rack. Broil according to recipe, detach cord, and serve food. Let broiler cool before washing. Never immerse electric element in water.

Food Combinations	Distance of pan from heat	Total Broiling Time in minutes
Bacon (do eggs on griddle)	1″ (1st shelf down)	6-8 minutes
Calf's liver and orange slices	3″ (2nd shelf down)	6-10 minutes
Cheeseburgers and tomato	5″ (bottom shelf)	8-12 minutes
Chicken See Recipe 158		
Fish See Recipe 156		
Grapefruit Halves and Bananas	3″ (2nd shelf down)	8-10 minutes
Ham, uncooked, ½″ thick	3″ (2nd shelf down)	12-15 minutes
Hamburgers	3″ (2nd shelf down)	8-12 minutes
Lamb Chops See Recipe 157		
Sandwiches and Toast	5″ (bottom shelf)	6-10 minutes
Sausages and Canned Apricots	3″ (2nd shelf down)	12-16 minutes
Steaks, 1 inch thick	3″ (2nd shelf down)	10-12 rare 13-15 medium
Steaks, 1½ inches thick	3″ (2nd shelf down)	13-15 rare 16-18 medium
Toast, French (6 slices at once!)	5″ (bottom shelf)	5-8 minutes

HOW TO USE GRIDDLE TOP OF YOUR INFRA-RED BROILER: Preheat griddle 4 minutes. Brush with fat or margarine. Follow standard recipes for griddle cakes (2 minutes each side); hamburger patties (5-7 minutes each side); fully ripe or canned fruits (4 minutes per side). Your griddle keeps coffee and rolls warm.

HOW TO MANAGE: *Broil planked fish with peaches alongside; heat rolls on grill at same time.*

155   PLANKED SALMON STEAK SPECIAL

Total oven time: 14-18 minutes in preheated broiler
Set rack 4" from heat (usually 3rd shelf down)   *4 servings*

SALMON, POTATO AND MUSHROOM PLANK
1½ pounds salmon steak
4 mashed potato mounds, seasoned
4 large mushroom caps
Salt and pepper
Butter

Arrange salmon on greased large plank or ovenproof platter. Place potatoes and mushrooms around it. Season with salt and pepper. Dot generously with butter. Broil until flaky.

BROILED PEACH HALVES: Combine 2 tablespoons peach sirup and 4 tablespoons brown sugar. Spread over 4 canned peach halves and into hollows. Broil alongside fish.

HOT CLOVERLEAF ROLLS WITH LEMON BUTTER: Combine 2 tablespoons butter or margarine, 2 teaspoons lemon juice, 2 tablespoons grated lemon rind. Spread over cloverleaf rolls. Keep hot on griddle (top of broiler).

156   HOW TO BROIL FISH

Total oven time: 10-14 minutes in preheated broiler
Set rack 3" from heat (usually 2nd shelf down)

Broil small fish whole. Cut large ones into steaks ½" to 1" thick, or open them flat. Butter and broil on double-thick aluminum foil or in greased shallow pan. Combine ½ cup butter, 1 tablespoon chopped parsley, 2 tablespoons lemon juice, heat in butter pipkin or custard cup placed on grill, and serve with broiled fish. Do not turn fillets; turn thick slices once.

HOW TO MANAGE: *Put sauerkraut in shallow pan, cover with rack, add chops and potatoes.*

157   QUICK GRILL FEATURING APRICOT LAMB CHOPS

Total oven time: 18-22 minutes in preheated broiler
Set rack 4" from heat (usually 3rd shelf down)   *4 servings*

LAMB CHOPS WITH APRICOT STUFFING

4 lamb chops, 1½" thick
3 tablespoons butter or margarine
3 tablespoons chopped celery
½ cup soft bread crumbs
¼ cup cooked minced apricots
Salt and pepper
3 tablespoons oil

Cut extra fat from chops, and slash edges to prevent curling. Cut a pocket in the side of each chop. Melt butter in skillet, cook celery until soft, turn in other ingredients, and use to stuff pocket. Fasten with picks. Sprinkle chops with oil, broil on rack in shallow pan until done as you like them, turning once.

SPICY SAUERKRAUT: Sprinkle 2 tablespoons wine vinegar over 2 cups sauerkraut. Heat in shallow pan under rack containing chops.

POTATO PUFFS: Spread alongside chops in double-thick aluminum foil. Turn together.

BROILING TIME FOR LAMB CHOPS

Thickness of chop	Time in minutes	Distance of pan from heat
½ inch	7-10	3 inches
¾ inch	9-12	3 inches
1 inch	12-16	4 inches
1½ inches	18-22	4 inches
2 inches	19-24	5 inches

(Preheat broiler for 4 minutes; allow maximum times for well-done.)

FOR DESSERT: *Sprinkle bought cherry pie with nutmeg. Heat in broiler for 10 minutes. Hot pie is tops in flavor!*

158 SUNDAY CHICKEN BARBECUE

Total oven time: 35-45 minutes in preheated broiler
Set rack 4" from heat (usually 3rd shelf down) **4 servings**

OLD-FASHIONED CHICKEN BARBECUE

1 quartered broiling chicken, about 3 pounds
½ cup oil
¼ cup vinegar
1 clove garlic, mashed
2 tablespoons grated onion
1 teaspoon salt
¼ teaspoon pepper

Wash chicken. Combine other ingredients, pour over bird and let stand at least 1 hour. Put chicken and sauce in pan (not on rack since chicken should bake in its own juice) skin side down. Broil until crisp and tender, turning once. A family favorite, and easy too!

CHILI CORN ON COB: Brush cooked or canned corn on cob with plenty of melted butter, season with salt, pepper, chili powder. Add 10 minutes before chicken is done.

BROILED TOMATOES: Cut slice from stem end of chunky tomatoes. Brush with oil, sprinkle with garlic salt and dill, pushing seasoning into tomato. Add with corn.

PARSLEY FRENCH BREAD: Slice a loaf of French bread almost to the bottom. Brush melted butter and parsley into each slice and on top. Toast for few minutes while you are passing chicken.

Index

About your broiler griddle, 123
About your roaster-oven, 8
Anchovy fingers, 20

Baked eggs, cheese and pasta, 28-35
Beef
   carbonado, 54
   caraway Swiss steak with roast potatoes, 50
   chipped beef brownies, 20
   individual beef and liver loaves, 53
   Italian beef rolls, 52
   juicy slow pot roast, 49
   calf's liver casserole
   meat pie parmigiana, 51
   musaca, 55
   old-fashioned country loaf, 51
   quick pot roast, 49
   roast beef, 48
   tangy barbecued liver, 57
   veal loaf and vegetable casserole, 58
   veal marengo, 59
Biscuits
   bacon, 101
   buttermilk, 101
   cheese, 101
   filled, 101
   orange marmalade, 101
   parsley, 101
   pinwheel, 101
   plain, 101
   rich cream, 101
Breads
   banana tea, 98
   buttermilk corn meal rolls, 99
   date-nut, 98
   easy oatmeal, 100
   empanadas, 100
   old-fashioned sour cream corn, 99
   Parker House rolls, 103
   popovers that pop, 102
   prune and apricot nut loaf, 98

Cakes
   banana layer, 103, 104
   quick chocolate, 104
   upside-down pineapple, 105
   walnut and apricot loaf, 106
Casserole
   calf's liver, 56
   creamy oatmeal breakfast, 25
   Louisiana sweet potato, 95
   musaca, 55
   New Orleans lamb and bean, 62
   of eggs à la king, 29
   of Spanish rice, 33
   onion and apple, 90
   orange-coconut chicken, 78
   pork chop, apple and spaghetti, 65
   quick tuna and mushroom, 45
   veal loaf and vegetable, 58
Casseroles featuring eggs, 28
Cheese
   and nut wafers, 23
   cottage, and onion fondue, 32
   luncheon bake, 30
   Roquefort, 22
   soufflé for six, 32
   sticks, 23
   Sunday supper of olives, rice, and —, 31
   Swiss cheese and onion tart, 21
   roll, 21
Chicken
   barbecued baked, 74
   Chinese pepper, 79
   coq au vin, 77
   easy oven-fried, 73
   fabulous curry, 82
   favorite, and rice loaf, 80
   liver, mushroom and bacon skewers, 18
   old-fashioned, and ham potpie, 81
   orange-coconut casserole, 78
   pie with perfect crispy crust, 81

pollo con arroz, 75
savory stuffed drumsticks, 76
Sunday barbecue, 126
Cookies, 106-107

Desserts
apple-noodle charlotte, 112
apricot fluff, 113
baked apples in maple syrup, 112
baked bananas, 114
banana-pecan pudding, 114
banana souffléed, in shell, 114
coconut cup custard, 115
compote of fruit, oven, 118
country rice pudding, 117
lemon chiffon pudding, 115
orange-coconut pudding, 116
Oregon apple pudding, 113
pineapple brown Betty, 116
prunes au vin, 118
prune soufflé, 118
rhubarb and pineapple meringue, 117
Duckling baked in cranberry sauce, 83

Eggs
and walnuts, 28
casserole of, à la king, 29
Cuban, 28
curried diablo, 30
Florentine, 28
with chicken livers, 28

Fish
baked bass with mushroom stuffing, 38
celery-salmon scallop, 41
fillet of flounder with grapes, 40
fillets in almond sauce, 45
how to broil, 124
quick tuna and mushroom casserole, 45
rolled flounder fillets, 40
salmon steak special, planked, 124

Gnocchi, 35

Ham
and mushrooms in pastry shells, 19
baked glazed, 67
pineapple rolls with cheese toast, 68
How to care for your roaster-oven, 9, 10

Lamb
chops, apricot, 125
New Orleans, and bean casserole, 62
ragout with pimento biscuits, 61
roast in pineapple marinade, 60
Lasagna, 34
Liver and bacon roll, 20

Mushrooms, 19

Pies
deep-dish blueberry, 109
flaky shells, 107
Louisiana pecan, 109
spicy apple, 108
Pork
barbecued spareribs in piquant sauce, 69
Chinese roast, 63
chop, apple and spaghetti casserole, 65
chops and vegetables in sour cream, 66
curried apricot chops, 66
perfect baked bacon, 64
spareribs in apple juice, 69
stuffed tenderloin, 64
succulent roast, 63

Rice, 33

Shellfish
baked clams California, 39
deviled crabs, 39
golden brown scallops, 42
oyster casserole, 44
oysters oven-fried, 42
and shrimp Jambalaya, 43
Soup
onion, 24
zuppa del paes, 24

Time tables
beef, 48
ham, 67
lamb, 60, 125
poultry, 72
Turkey, roast stuffed, 72

Vegetables, 86-96